A

History of Upton,

NORFOLK.

BY

PERCIVAL OAKLEY HILL,

VICAR,

*Member of the Norfolk and Norwich Archæological Society, and
Diocesan Inspector of Schools.*

WITH AN INTRODUCTION AND "HISTORY OF THE MANOR
OF UPTON" BY

WALTER RYE.

"How can the present yield fruit, or the future have promise, except their
roots be fixed in the past."—*Dr. Arnold.*

Norwich:

AGAS H. GOOSE, RAMPANT HORSE STREET.

1891.

FONT IN UPTON CHURCH.

TO

THE HONOURABLE AND RIGHT REVEREND

JOHN THOMAS,

LORD BISHOP OF NORWICH,

THESE PAGES

ARE (WITH HIS PERMISSION)

GRATEFULLY DEDICATED

BY

THE AUTHOR.

PREFACE.

IN offering the following pages as a contribution to the Parish Histories of Norfolk, I may state that its publication has not been hastily undertaken; for some years I have collected materials from many sources, but cannot, even now, lay claim to completeness for the little work, and am conscious of shortcomings, partly my own, and partly owing to lack of information which I have been unable to obtain.

My grateful thanks are due to Mr. Walter Rye, for his Introduction, and interesting sketch of the chief manor (pages 5 to 12); to the Rev. W. Hudson, for kindly criticism; to Dr. Bensly for permission to search the Diocesan Records; to the Ven. Archdeacon of Norwich, and Mr. W. Overbury, for access to the Archdeacon's Registry; to Mr. Henry Gales, Medallist of the Royal Academy, for the time and ability he has bestowed in illustrating the book; and to Mr. Tallack for notes of interest, and most of the extracts of wills.

In my search among the archives of the Archdeaconry I have been impressed by what they reveal of the deplorable state of the churches in the Blofield Deanery some fifty years after the Reformation. The swing of the pendulum appears to have carried men from the extreme of superstitious reverence for the church and its ornaments, to the opposite extreme of slovenliness and irreverence, nay, of gross and abominable neglect.

In Upton the floor of the chancel was so disturbed by the removal of the pre-Reformation altar, that as late as 1597 the Archdeacon found it necessary to order "the pavement of the said chauncell where the hygh altar stoode, to be repayred and comelie paved."

In 1604 the Archdeacon found "the chauncell there in great ruyne and decaie, so yt the fowles and vermyn come in and do greatly defile the same. The grave of Edmond Brownes is as yet uncovered, culpa uxoris sue."

The churchyard also suffered desecration, for at the same Visitation this entry occurs: "There is a sawing pitt made in the churchyard there, verie unseemlie, and in making thereof they digged up the dead."

That Upton was by no means an exceptional case is shewn by the following extracts from the Archdeacon's books for the years 1601 and 1603-4.

Beighton.—"Pasch., 1604. The steple there is to be new builded, the one half thereof is built, the other undone, so yt it lieth open and the vermyn and fowles come into the same and defile the church."

Blofield.—"The communion table there is

unsufficient. 1601 : The church is to be decked with Scripture on the walles."

Braydeston.—" The porch there is uncovered in the roofe. The church is annoyed (?) with a heape of chips and ould tymber, very unseemlie. The church wyndowes in many places are broken."

Brundall.—" The chauncell windowes are broken in the glasse."

Buckenham.—" There want a comelie carpet for the communion table. The windowes of the church in many places there decaied and broken. The cloath of the comunion table is full of holes. The porch wanteth thacking."

Freethorpe.—" They have no service one Wednesdays and fridays as they ought to have."

Halvergate.—" There is a muckhill lying att the church porch. The belles there in decaie and cannot be ronge."

Hemblington.—" It rayneth into the church betweene the leade and the thatch."

Limpenhoe.—" The comunion table cloth is not sufficient, they are to provide a new. There is a grave in the church uncovered."

Lingwood.—"The pavement of the chauncel decaied. The chauncell there to be comelie whited. The dore of the said chauncell to be made new or the old dore to be sufficiently amended."

Plumstead Parva.—"The leades of the church are to be amended. There want a comelie table of ye tenne commandements of Almightie God."

Postwick.—"They are to prepare a new comunion table."

· *Reedham.*—"There is a donghill lying hard by the porch."

Walsham St. Lawrence.—"The bible is rent and torne in many places. There is a muck heape lieth in the churchyard before the north dore."

Walsham St. Mary.—"A heape of stones lieth in the church, verie unseemlye."

Wickhampton.—"The church there is unthached. The churchyard is unfenced."

The Visitation records also indicate that in many parishes public morality was as dilapidated

as were the churches. A few examples will suffice
for illustration :

Acle, 1586.—" Johannes Downinge, no^r (notatur)
ut sequitur, viz., that he mayntayne mennes
servauntes to plaie at cardes and Tables in his
howse on the Saboth daie in eveninge praier
tyme, viz., one Gryme of Walsham and fower
mennes servants the Sondaie before Michaelmasse
daie."

Halvergate, 1585.—" Richardus Lacey de Boyton
for drivinge his carte on the saboathe daye to the
town of Halvergate with hearing."

Limpenhoe, 1601.—" Nichs. Dawling, no^r, that he
is greatly suppocsed to use the devillish practyse
of witchcraft."

Upton.—" Creake, no^r, for prophaning the saboth
day by carting upon the Saboth in harvest last."

Many similar entries occur, and charges were
often brought of a still graver nature.

With these facts before us, and with the knowledge of what our venerable and beloved Church
passed through in the troublous times of the
Commonwealth, and the lethargic Georgian period,

we cannot be too thankful for the Victorian age of reverent care for the externals of worship, and the evidence of spiritual activity and power so manifest in present day developments of the Church's life.

P. O. H.

Upton Vicarage,
January, 1891.

INTRODUCTION.

THE author of the following excellent description of a Norfolk parish asked me, why I know not, to write a page or so of introduction to it, which I very willingly agreed to do, on one condition only, which he has faithfully carried out, that he should agree to print all the inscriptions in the church, and full notes of all those in the churchyard.[1]

---

[1] This having been done, makes Upton the 104th Norfolk church, the monuments in and about which are now preserved from the fantastic tricks of future "restorers." Those already printed are the inscriptions for all the 103 parishes in Holt, Happing, North Erpingham, and Tunstead.

All who read this book will, I think, agree
with me, that it is almost a perfect model for
incumbents of other parishes, who, at compara-
tively small individual trouble and expense, might
often write the history of their parishes, and so,
by united effort, in time complete a history of the
county, which would be of the highest possible
value; and I trust, that after so successful a
début, Mr. Hill may soon present us with equally
good accounts of Fishley and other adjoining
parishes.

To the antiquary proper, whose desires are like
those of the daughter of the horse leech, and who
is never satisfied with anything, however nearly it
may approach perfection, the absence of more
extracts from the parish registers will be regretted.
The local topographer should (especially when, as
in the present case, he has the custody of the
register, and could easily do so) give, at all events,
all the marriages before 1700; and there was no
special reason why the names of voters in the
Poll Books of 1714 and 1802 should have been
given, and those of 1734, 1768, 1806, 1817, &c.,

have been omitted. After most of the sheets had been sent me I found myself able to supply the author, from my own collection, with an interesting lease of the rectory from the bishop, dated 11th July, 1664, in which the vicar's right to his military-sounding "sixpence a day" is fully acknowledged.

The possibility of the vicarage garden having been an Anglo-Saxon burial ground is pointed out by Mr. Hill on p. 98, and, I think with considerable force, while the Norman piscina discovered in 1885 is well figured on p. 50.

It is refreshing to find the author adopting the reasonable derivation of the place-name "Up-ton," instead of the rather fantastic idea of the late Rev. Geo. Munford.

On p. 38 is recorded a very interesting case of so-called brawling in church, in which a man was punished for carrying a bone on which a robin redbreast and a wren were hung, into the church, on Christmas Day, 1612. There is little doubt that we have here an early reference of the "carrying of the wren,"[2] best known in Ireland, on and about St. Stephen's Day (26th December); Christmas Day, being of course, the eve of St. Stephen; a curious instance of how records of early customs may be accidentally preserved.

WALTER RYE.

[2] Accompanied by men singing,—

"The wren, the wren, the king of all birds,
St. Stephen's Day was caught in the furze, &c."

CONTENTS.

ILLUSTRATIONS.

History of the Parish of Upton.

CHAPTER I.

Of the Parish: its Name, Anglo-Saxon Origin, and Sketch of Manorial History.

OF the twenty-nine parishes in England and Wales bearing the name of Upton, one only is situate in Norfolk.[1] The name indicates an Anglo-Saxon origin for the place whose recorded history begins nearly 1,000 years ago. In *Domesday Book* the parish is called OPTUNA, OPTUNE, VPTUNA, and VPTUNE; in the twelfth century the name occurs as UPPETONA;

[1] Upton is in the Hundred of South Walsham, and Deanery of Blofield.

B

a later form is OPTON; in 1556 the spelling is given in the *Institution Book* as UPPTON; and on the Communion cup (temp. Elizabeth) it is spelt VPTVN.

The Rev. George Munford, in his *Local Names in Norfolk*, suggests the following as the derivation of the name Upton :—" The prefix is the personal name Up, Upp, Uppe. A person of the name of Up, Uppe, was the founder of the family called the Uppings. The Anglo-Saxon word Up, Upp, Uppe, signifies high, tall, and from these words it might be thought the village was situated on an elevation, but it is not so. The personal name, however, may have been applied to one who was *tall*, or who was high in station. *Ton*, Anglo-Saxon *Tun*, an enclosed space, as a garden, a court, a district, a town. Not a town, however, in the modern acceptation of the term, but rather a tract of land enjoyed by a community. Thus *Tun*, in districts, generally expresses what we should rather call a village, or a property with the buildings of the peasants thereon ; and it might, strictly speaking, consist of a single homestead, nay, according to the old law, it might be a tun though there were not a house standing in the district."

I cannot accept the above writer's derivation of the prefix, for not only is there no trace, so far as I know, of anyone of the name of Up or Upping having had any connection with Upton, but a part of the parish *is* quite sufficiently elevated to win for it the name *Up*ton. The earliest invaders would naturally take the course of the Bure valley —then an arm of the sea—from the open sea at Yarmouth, and would find the high ground of Upton suitable for a settlement. A century after the Norman Conquest it was found desirable to build the church on the upland overlooking the tide-covered marshes, so as to be well out of the reach of exceptional tides, which, no doubt, visited a great part of the present site of the village. That the Bure valley was subject to inundation as late as the reign of James I., is evident from the following extract from Mason's *History of Norfolk*, vol. i. p. 252 :—

"In the seventh year of this reign, an Act of Parliament was passed for 'the speedy recovery of many thousand acres of marsh ground, and other grounds, within the counties of Norfolk and Suffolk, lately surrounded by the sea.' There had been great inundations between the town of Great Yarmouth and Hasborough, which had broken down and washed away the cliffs and higher grounds, and made breaches so wide that the sea broke in at every tide, especially when high winds prevailed, greatly to the injury of husbandmen. The influx of salt water also inflicted much injury

on the fishings of the rivers, creeks, and other
places, which had customarily given employment
to many poor men, and had supplied many
markets." Amongst other places mentioned as
endangered were South Walsham, Upton, Acle,
Tilby (Filby), &c.

Blomefield's *History of Norfolk* gives a record
of Upton in Anglo-Saxon times: "Twenty-six
socmen[2] held a carucate[3] and an half of land,
thirty-five acres of meadow, and three carucates;
the town was one leuca[4] long and one broad, and
paid 2s. gelt.[5] The king and the earl had the
soc and sac over all their socmen, except seven,
who had the soc under their protection or com-
mendation. . . . In Opton was a socman with
twelve acres, valued at 2s., and the soc of these
belonged to the hundred."

The king here referred to was Edward the

---

[2] Tenure by socage—"The tenant pays his rent by a certain
number of day's labour, in husbandry, or other service."—*England
Displayed.* "From Anglo-Saxon *soc;* the privilege of holding a
court in a district. A tenure of lands in England by the performance
of certain and determinate service."—*Annandale.*

[3] Carucate—"About 100 acres."—*Mason.*

[4] "Leuca, derived from the Celtic *leong* or *leak*, a milestone,
means twelve quarantines, or a mile."—Goulburn's *History of
Norwich Cathedral.*

[5] Danegelt, the ancient tax levied to maintain forces to oppose the
Danes.

Confessor (1042), and the earl, Ralph Guader, Earl of Norfolk. William the Conqueror appears to have dispossessed Earl Ralph of the lordship or manor of Upton, and placed it under the care of Godric, his Dapifer or Steward, who is said to have been an ancestor of the de Calthorpes. Godric also seems to have owned land in Upton, as well as his royal master.

The following sketch of the manor has been kindly written for these pages by one who has made much research into the intricacies of subinfeudation.

HISTORY OF THE MANOR OF UPTON.

By Mr. Walter Rye.

From *Domesday* it was clear there were two manors at Upton—the king's and the earl's (Ralph Guader's). The latter, no doubt, came into the king's hands on the forfeiture of his estate, after his rebellion, and probably both manors merged into one, and were held together.[6]

---

[6] It is possible, however, that the interest vested in 1515 in the Countess of Suffolk in a manor here was the Crown Manor, for Sir Robert Southwell, who we shall see then held the main manor, is said to have held of her—though, of course, he may have had an interest in both manors. Or her manor may have been the Earl's Manor. Whatever this manor was, Henry VIII. seems to have granted it to *Anne of Cleves* about 1540, and later on it belonged to *Charles Brandon*, Earl of Suffolk.

There is some confusion as to the early ownership of what we may call the actual manor, by
which I mean that which held its courts at Upton,
and whose tenants were the tillers of the soil, and
not the shadowy manor or manors of the superior
or intermediate lords.

Blomefield says (p. 133) "that Henry II. seized
it as an escheat because *Andrew le Boteler* refused
to perform his services"; but I do not think the
family of le Boteler, or Pincerna as it is sometimes
called, had any interest in the place so early as
the reign of Henry II. (1154—1189).

The true version is probably that given by the
Inquisition in the Hundred Rolls, which was taken
in 1275, and which states that the manor of
Upton, with its members, viz., in Fixley (Fishley)
and Walsham, were seized as an escheat into the
king's hands, because *Andrew le Buscari*, who held
it, would not do his services, and that King Henry
"the Elder" granted it to

Ranulph de Glanville (being in extent ten
librates of land,[7] and that Ranulph gave (*i.e.,*
subinfeoffed at half a knight's fee, see pp. 20, 21)
the manor to

Reyner le Sirene or *le Sirgne,* who gave it with

---

[7] This is how I read "decem libr' terre," though *Add. MSS.*
8843, fo. 46, speaks of its having been granted in consideration of
£10.

his sister Catherine in marriage to Nicholas le Boteler, sen., of Wickmere.

This Reyner is, no doubt, the Reiner "de Wirtonesham," to whom Henry confirmed the manor on the petition of Ralph de Glanville. His real surname was, no doubt, "de Wytlesham." Reiner de Wytlesham's son William, as it will be seen later on, marrying Beatrice le Botiler.

Nicholas le Botiler or Pincerna, as we have seen, took the manor by right of his wife, *Catherine.* In 1210 he held it at half a knight's fee of Hugh de Auberville, who is said to have held the same in capite.[8] Ranulph de Glanville's interest having meanwhile passed to Hugh de Auberville, who was his grandson, his daughter Matilda having married William de Auberville.

Catherine le Botiler, the daughter and heiress of Nicholas, married

Thomas Rocelin, who, at the time of the inquest set out in the Hundred Rolls (1275), claimed free warren in his demesnes in Upton, but the jury stated they did not know by what warrant.

Blomefield, on the other hand, says that Nicholas le Botiler died without issue (possibly he means that his daughter, Catherine Rocelin, died without issue), and that his widow (second wife ?) *Beatrix*

---

[8] Red Book of the Exchequer, fo. 116, quoted by Le Neve, *Addl. MSS.* 8843, fo. 46.

afterwards married William, son of Reyner de
Wythelesham,[9] who held it for her life. This
seems true, for we find them conveying by fine
their interest therein to *Guy de Boutetourt* (*Feet
of Fines for Norfolk*, 2nd Edward I., 1294, No. 21).
This was, apparently, the first interest Guy, who
afterwards secured the whole manor, had in
Upton.

Somehow or another the manor came to two
coheiresses, whose very Christian and surnames
are unknown, but who were probably nieces of
Nicholas le Botiler, and daughters of the Richard
le Botiler who had something to do with the
advowson in 23rd Henry III. (1238-9).

These heiresses married :—

1.   *Adam de Brancaster*, who sold his moiety of
the manor of Wickmere, and probably of Upton
also, in 1289 to *William* fil' William [del Park] *de
Heveningham*, and his moiety of North Burlingham
and Fishley to Guy de Botetourt.—*Blom. Norf.* vi.
p. 224.

2.   *William de St. Clere*, who is said to have
also sold his moiety to *William de Heveningham*.
Felicia de St. Clere, his widow, claimed an interest
in Upton in 14th Edward I. (1286).

---

[9] As to the corruption, Wirtonesham, *see supra*. At just the
same time there was a William, son of Reyner of Felmingham.—
Feet of Fines, 3rd and 4th Edward I., No. 64.

By 1287, *Guy de Botetourt*,[1] who it will be remembered had bought up the life interest of the widow of a former owner, in 1272 seems to have acquired the whole manor, for he claimed the right of frankpledge in that year, and had a grant of a market and fair here in 1302.

This manor probably passed in the same way as Cantley, which Guy settled in 1305 (33rd Edw. I.) on his son.

William de Botetourt, who is probably the William de Botetourt who, with his wife Matilda, were living in 12th Edw. II. (1319).

In 1323 an extent was taken of (*i.a.*) the manor of Upton, belonging to *Thomas de Botetourt* and Johanna his wife,[2] who was sister and coheiress of John, Lord Somery.

In 1358 *John Buttetourt* of Welney (it is not clear who he was or how he held the manors, unless he was the uncle-trustee), settled the manors of Upton and Cantley on another

John Buttetourt, and the latter's wife Matilda,

---

[1] It will be noticed I follow the usual spelling, but I must doubt if the name should not be read Botecourt. Buttecourt and Buttencourt occur in different copies of the Roll of Battle Abbey. The family came from Cantley, of which manor Roger de Botecourt had a grant by fine in 13th Henry III. (1228), and the pedigree, which deserves careful revision, would seem to run as in the chart showing the descent of the manor.

[2] Inq. p. m. 16th Edward II., No. 56, i. 304 a.

daughter of John de Grey of Retherfield (*Feet of Fines*). He left a daughter and heiress,

Jocosa or Joyce Buttetourt, who married Sir Hugh Burnel, who held the manor in her right, 2nd Henry IV. (1400). In the previous year they had settled Upton and Cantley, their trustees being John Rome, cler', and others (*Feet of Fines, Norf.,* 1st Henry IV. No. 3).

She died without issue, and according to Blomefield (vii. p. 229) John Rome, her trustee, conveyed Upton and Cantley to

Sir Thomas Erpingham; but I cannot trace that this celebrated man ever had any interest in the manor, except, possibly, as trustee.

It ought to have passed through Joyce Boutetourt's or Burnel's sister, *Margaret* Burnel, who married *John de Sutton;* who, no doubt, was the Sir John de Sutton of Wivenho who held a manor in Rockland Tofts by right of his wife *Margaret* in 1359 (*Bl. Norf.* i. p. 479.)

In 1433 *Nicholas Wichingham* died lord of Upton, but how he had acquired the manor I do not know. By the tabular pedigree[3] facing p. 5, however, it will be seen that he was the son of Sir William de Wichingham by *Margaret*, who Norris thinks was the heiress of the de Antingham family, but who may either have been this Margaret Sutton,

[1] Chiefly from Norris MS. History of North Erpingham (penes W. Rye).

formerly Burnel, and have married de Witchingham secondly; or her daughter of the same Christian name.

He was Sheriff of Norfolk in 1405-6, and by Alice, his first wife, had

William de Wichingham, his son and heir, who no doubt died without issue, for, both here and at Cantley, he was succeeded by his half-brother Edmund, by his father's second wife Joan, who, rather than her mother-in-law, I think, may have been the heiress of Antingham.

Edmund Wichingham, who of Woodrising was lord in 1434, and by his wife Alice, daughter and heiress of John Fastolf of Fishley, had issue four daughters, of whom one,

Amy Wichingham, married Sir Richard Southwell, and was father of

Sir Robert Southwell, who is said to have held the manor of the Countess of Suffolk, about 1515.

How it got into the king's hands by 1545 I do not know; but in that year (5th May, 37th Hen. VIII.) it was granted to *Sir Richard*[4]

[4] Sir Richard Southwell, Knight, *cir.* 1545. This Sir Richard was grandfather of the poet, Robert Southwell. Blomefield says of Sir Richard—"He was a great favourite of King Henry VIII.; one of the visitors, appointed by him, of the monasteries in Norfolk on their suppression; of the Privy Council to that king, Edward VI., and Queen Mary; Master of the Ordnance and Armory; one of the Executors to Henry VIII.; and High Steward of the Duchy of Lancaster."

Southwell (nephew of the late lord, and son of his brother Francis by Dorothy Tendring, his wife), with Wendling, Kerdiston, &c. He is said to have "conveyed" [surrendered?] it to the king in the following year.

In 1546 the king settled it on the Dean, &c., of Christ Church, Oxford,[5] who held it till quite recently, when it was sold to

William Waters, Esq., about 1822, from whom it passed to

John Waters, Esq., about 1859, whose trustees succeeded to it in 1876.

OWNERS OF OTHER MANORIAL OR PROPERTY RIGHTS.

The Abbot and Convent of Holm, temp. Edward the Confessor.

Godric the Dapifer, temp. William the Conqueror.

Will de Stutevile, op. se 4to. die versus Roger de Cressy de placito capiendi Chyrograph suum de fine facto inter eos de terr. in Upton et at ptcita apud Bedf. Cor. Willo. de Rupe et sociis Anno 25 Henr. III., Oct. 1mo.—*Add. MSS.* 8843, fo. 46.

Henry de Cat and Margery his wife, recovered

---

[5] Upton Manor, yearly value £26. 16s. 8¼d., to St. Frideswide, Oxford.—*Dugdale's Mon.* ii. 171.

of Ralph de Rothing pasture land in Upton, 1288. —*Bl. Norf.* v. 1495.

Sunderland Hall, or Brome Manor, in South Walsham, had rights in Upton (Petronilla, widow of Sir Roger de Brome, 1304).—*Bl. Norf.* v. 1496.

Will. de Bergh held lands here,[6] 43 Edward III.

Stephen Fowlhand of Upton and Henry Mountford of South Walsham confirmed to Peter Erle of Upton, Tho. atte Den of the same, and Geffrey Erle of North Burlingham,[7] one acre of land in Northmarsh in Upton, 1410.

Elizabeth, wife of John Bray of Norwich, owned rights in Upton belonging to her manor of Mount or Mill-hill in Wickhampton and other parishes, 1473.—*Bl. Norf.* v. 1493.

Elizabeth, widow of John Holditch leaves all her lands in Upton to her son Robert Holditch, 1524. Robert Moneyman conveyed land here to Robert Holditch, temp. Henry VIII.—*Bl. Norf.* v. 1474-5.

Simon Owghlawe owns land in Upton, afterwards possessed by Thomas Clere, 1542. Thomas Clere also had land here which formerly belonged to John Reynes of Acle.—*Court of Wards and Liveries,* vi. 129.

---

[6] *Add. MSS.* 8843, pp. 118—122.

[7] Abutting on ye land of the manor, Sunderland Hall.—*Add. MSS.*, 8843, pp. 118—122.

Richard Fulmerston, Esq., held a grant of lands in Upton of Weybridge Priory, Acle (the Upton temporalities of which priory, at the Dissolution, were valued at 20*d.*), *circ.* 1547.—*Bl. Norf.* v. 1492.

Robert Rownce held land in Upton, respecting which there was a Chancery suit, temp. Elizabeth.

Mauritius Adolphus Newton Stark, Esq., lord of the manor of Beighton in Upton, in right of his wife, 1799.

The Vansittart family owned an estate, now the property of Miss Coventry, Stoke Severn Rectory, 1890.

P. B. Bellin, Esq., and Mrs. Downing Farrar, also have an estate here.

Mr. S. Munford, nephew of the author of *Local Names in Norfolk*, is also a landowner.

[For other ownership rights *vide* extracts of wills, Chapter VII.]

The Parish Award, dated 1802, recognises rights in Upton of the manors of—1, Upton; 2, South Walsham; 3, Cattishall in South Walsham; 4, Chamery Hall in South Walsham; 5, Rowthinghall in South Walsham; 6, Ranworth and Panxworth; 7, Beighton.

In the Award, nine public and fifteen private roads are given. Over the latter the Commissioners have granted to the rector and vicar a right of way, as follows:—"We do hereby declare

that the said several private roads are also hereby
set out and appointed for the use and convenience
of the Right Reverend the Lord Bishop of Ely
and his successors, owners of the Rectory of
Upton, and of his and their lessees for the time
being of the said rectory, and of the said John
Oldershaw, clerk, vicar of the vicarage of Upton
aforesaid, and of his successors, vicars of the said
vicarage for the time being for ever."

The following are short notes of the earlier Feet
of Fines in which the Parish of Upton is
mentioned. The full references will be
found in Rye's *Calendar of Norfolk Fines.*

7th Richard I. Stephen de Ludinge *v.* *Robert
le Wile, of a virgate in Upton—being a partition.

18th Henry III. Magr. Hugh de Upton *v.*
Magr. *Walter de Upton, in Upton.

23rd Henry III. Richard le Butilier *v.* *the
Prior of Buttel, of the advowson of Upton.

25th Henry III. *Cristiana, widow of Thomas
de S'co Audomero, *v.* Simon de Criketoft, in
Walsham, . . . Upton, Randewurth, Hemlingham,
Beigheton, Mouton, and Wikhampton.

38th Henry III. William de Nicole *v.* *John
fil' William le Lord and Maria his wife, in Upton.

11th and 12th Edward I. *Bartholomew fil'

Radulphus de Somerton, by J'no de Livermere, v. Constance de Somerton, by J'no de Walcote, in Randeworth, Pankesford, and Upton.

14th Edward I. Thomas fil' Gerard de Redham and Rosa his wife v. *Ralph de Redham and Margaret his wife, in Fysshele, Upton, Akele, Northbirlingham, Frenthorp, and Burgh in Fleg. (Wydo Butecurte app. clam.)

14th Edward-I. Katherine fil' Walter Buckeskin v. *Katherine, the wife of Walter Buckeskyn, in Fisshele, Upton, Frethorp, Northbyrlingham, and Burg in Fleg.

33rd Edward I. William fil' Nicholas Rydel v. *Nicholas Rydel, by Randolf de Trous, in Wroxham, Rakheyth, Crostweyt, Beston, Bastwyk, Felthorp, Taverham, Attebrig, and Upton.

34th Edward I. *Robert fil' Maurice de Upton and Margaret his wife, by Randolf de Trous, v. Galfridus Cote of Breydeston, by Nicholas de Blofeld, in Upton, Fisshele, North Birlingham, and South Walsham. (Guydo Butecurte and William fil' James de Lincoln app. clam.)

35th Edward I. Nicholas Bukeskyn, by John de Friselond, v. *William Cayly and Katherine his wife, by Galfridus de Snetesham, in Fisshele, Upton, Frethorp, North Birlyngham, Burgh, and Fleg, which Katherine, the wife of Walter Buckeskyn, holds for life.

2nd Edward II. *Willm. Gerberge de Wyk-hampton and Johanna his wife *v.* Willm. de Corton and Clement de Stalham, in Wykhampton, Halv'gate, Tunstall, Ocle, Beyeghton, Mouton, Frethorp, Redham, Lympenhowe, Possewyk, Castre, Fisshele, Upton, and Cantele. (Robt. le Chaumberleyn and Hawys his wife app. clam. Willm. de Halviriate app. clam.)

2nd Edward II. Peter Bukskyn *v.* *John fil' Gerard de Redham and Rosa his wife, in Upton, Fisshele, Acle, Northbirlyngham, and Burgh in Fleg.

5th Edward II. Thom. de Cokefeld *v.* *Rog. de Upton and Emma his wife, in Erlham and Costeseye.

13th Edward III. *John de Coulenge *v.* Nigel de Halle of Crungelthorp, in Upton.

16th Edward III. Roger Hardegrey, John de Berneye, Thos. de Bumpsted, and John Yemme, *v.* *Peter Buckeskyn of Fisshele, of the manor of Burghalle in Fisshele, and the advowson of Fisshele, and land in Fisshele, Upton, Acle, Mouton, Frethorp, Northbirlyngham, South Wal-sham, Letheryngsete, Bastwyk juxta Rande-worthe, Berton juxta Smalbergh, and Beston juxta Berton.

29th and 30th Edward III. John de Welle and Alicia his wife *v.* *John de Caston, Chivaler, and

C

Kath. his wife, in Southbirlyngham, Geyghton, Accle, Upton, Lyngwode, South Walsham, Northbirlyngham, and Bokenhamfferie.

30th Edward III., 2nd MS., No. 1, p. 199b. John Cook de Upton and Claricia ux. ej., an acre of land at Upton, as parcel of the manor of Fishley.

42nd Edward III. John de Eccles *v.* *John de Elyngham and Kath. his wife, in Northbirlyngham, Upton, Walsham, Randworth, Panxford, and Hemelyngton.

49th Edward III. Robt. Dersyng *v.* *Andrew Bely (C ?) and Felicia his wife, in Upton.

3rd Henry IV. Thomas atte Grene of Southwalsham, Adam atte Grene, and Nich. atte Grene, *v.* John Holere of Mouton and Agnes his wife, in Southwalsham and Upton.

7th and 8th Henry IV. Wm. Lyghtfote, clericus, and John Lyghtfote of Bokenhamferye, *v.* *Nich. Blome and Cecilia his wife, in Northbyrlyngham, Southbirlyngham, Hasyngham, Lyngewode, Strumpeshawe, Blofeld, Hemlyngton, and Upton.

23rd Henry VI. John Reynere of Acle, Lawrance Oky, Thos. Oky, and Robt. Walle, *v.* *Rich. Goggeman and Margery his wife, in Upton, Acle, and Beyton.

CHAPTER II.

Of the Church: its Foundation, Founder, Patrons, and Clergy.

EXTRACT from *Domesday Book* quoted in Tanner's MS., Diocesan Registry.
Upton, dd. St. Margaretæ.

Domesd. Appropriatur Priori et conv. de Buttlee præter vicariam. Estimatio Rectoriæ xxv marc. Procuratio vii⁸ viiᵈ ob. Synodalia p annum ii⁸ iiiiᵈ. Denarii S. Petri xviᵈ. Carvagium iiiᵈ.

Eccl(es)ia donata fuit canonicis de B. a Ran. Glanvil fundatore p Hen. II.

From *the King's Book*, from which the amounts of firstfruits are taken, date 1786. Upton V. (St. Margaret). Clear yearly value, £24; Episc.

2s. 4d.; Archidiac, 7s. 7½d.; Mon. Butteley, Propr. Bishop of Ely, p. i. King's books, £3.

Although it is probable that the spiritual wants of the parish were cared for in Anglo-Saxon times, we have no *evidence* of the existence of a church until the year 1171, when Ranulph de Glanville founded and built in Upton a Norman church, and attached it to his new Priory of Butley, Suffolk. I have transcribed the subjoined document from Dugdale's [8] *Monasticon Anglicanum*, which is of interest as. being the legal instrument by which King Henry II. confirmed De Glanville's deed of gift of the Manor of Upton to the De Wirtonesham family on a feudal tenure, and the church and its patronage to Butley Priory.

De Advocatione Ecclesiæ de Uppetona data per Ranulphum de Glanville, Canonicis de Butley. [9]

---

[8] The deed quoted by Dugdale is *Cartæ Antiquæ*, P. n. 32, Public Record Office.

[9] Concerning the patronage of the church of Upton, granted by Ranulph de Glanville to the Canons of Butley.

HENRY, by the grace of God, King of England, Duke of Normandy, Duke of Aquitaine, Count of Anjou, to the Archbishops, &c., greeting—

Be it known to you that (at the petition of Ranulph de Glanville) I have granted, and by this present charter have confirmed to Reyner de Wirtonesham and his heirs, the manor of Upton, with all things thereto belonging, which I gave to the aforesaid Ranulph and his heirs, for his service; and the said Ranulph hath granted and confirmed by his own charter to the aforesaid Reyner to hold to him

HENRICUS Dei gratia rex Angliæ, dux Normanniæ, Aquitaniæ, comes Andegaviæ, archiepiscopis, &c., salutem. Sciatis me ad petitionem Ranulfi de Glanvill concessisse, et præsenti cartâ confirmâsse Reinero de Wirtonesham, et hæredibus suis, manerium de Uppetona, cum omnibus pertinentiis suis, quod ego dedi prædicto Ranulfo, et hæredibus suis, pro servitio suo, et idem Ranulfus dedit et cartâ suâ confirmavit prædicto Reynero, tenendum sibi, et hæredibus suis, de eodem Ranulfo, et hæredibus suis, per servitium feodi dimidii militis, cum omnibus pertinentiis suis, exceptâ ecclesiâ ejusdem villæ, et ejus præsentatione quam prædictus Ranulfus dedit Deo et ecclesiæ beatæ Mariæ de Buttelia, et canonicis ibidem Deo servientibus, in perpetuam elemosinam. Quare volo, &c.

and his heirs, from the said Ranulph and his heirs, by service of half a knight's fee, with all things thereto belonging, except the church of that town and its presentation, which the aforesaid Ranulph gave in perpetual alms to God and the Church of the Blessed Mary of Butley, and to the Canons who serve God there. Wherefore I will, &c.

Witnesses—Hugo Murdach.
John Cummin.
Bertram de Verdune.
Michael Belet.
William de Bend.
Hugo de Crescey.
Robert, the son of Bernard.

At Pontefract.

Testibus—Hugone Murdach.
Johanne Cummin.
Bertramo de Verdune.
Michæle Belet.
Willielmo de Bend.
Hugone de Crescey.
Roberto filio Bernardi.
Apud Pontemfractum.

SEAL OF HENRY II.

It may be of interest to subjoin some particulars
of the life of Ranulph de Glanville, whose memory

should ever be kept green by the people of Upton, out of gratitude to the eminent founder of their church.

LIFE OF RANULPH DE GLANVILLE.

Ranulph, Ranulf, Ralph, or Randal de Glanville, "the father of English jurisprudence," was born at Stratford, in Suffolk; but the date of his birth is unknown. He made his principal residence in Yorkshire, where some of the large possessions of his wife, Bertha, daughter and heiress of Theobald de Valoins, Lord of Parham, were situate. Lord Campbell states that "under King Stephen he was receiver for the forfeited Earldom of Conan, and collector of the rents of the Crown in Yorkshire and Westmoreland." Belonging to a family distinguished for founding religious houses, Ranulph exceeded the munificence of his kindred. In 1171 he established the Priory of Black Canons, of the Order of S. Augustine, at Butley, Suffolk, dedicating it to the Blessed Virgin Mary. In the same year—according to Blomefield—he founded the Church of S. Margaret, Upton, building it in the prevailing Norman style of architecture. The manor of Upton had been granted to him by King Henry II., who had taken it from Andrew le Boteler as an escheat, upon the latter "refusing to perform the service due to the king."[1] On founding the church, de Glanville gave the patronage to the Prior and Canons of his new Priory of Butley, which chapter presented a succession of vicars to the benefice of Upton, down to the year 1533. In 1183, Ranulph de Glanville founded an abbey of Premonstratensian Canons at Leiston, Suffolk, in the neighbourhood of his birthplace; and performed a further work (which Blomefield notes) in establishing "an hospital in West Somerton, for the king's soul, his own, and that of Barta, his wife, for three lepers, and gave the care or guardianship of it to the said priory" (of Butley).[2]

On Henry II. going to Ireland in 1171, to assert his sovereignty over those parts of the sister isle which had been newly conquered, de Glanville appears as Ireland's friend in bringing his conspicuous ability to the aid of the king in settling solid legal foundations on which the new dominions might rest. A reviewer in *The Churchman* of January, 1890, thus writes:—"Henry organized

[1] Beside the manor of Upton he appears to have had manors at Roughton, Dickleburgh, Bawdsey, and Glosthorp, and was lord of Benhall, as well as of part of the lordship of West Somerton.

[2] William de Glanville founded Bromholm Priory, for Cluniac Monks, as a cell to Castleacre in 1113. Another member of the family, Robert or Roger de Glanville, in conjunction with the Countess Gundreda, his wife, founded the Benedictine Nunnery of Bungay in 1160.

the legal and municipal affairs of Ireland. Assize Courts date from his visit. Ranulf de Glanville, 'greatest and earliest of English lawyers,' was by his side, and his signature[3] can still be seen to the Dublin Charter of 1171, in *Chartæ Privilegia et Immunitates*, published by the Irish Record Office. But while he thus, during his brief stay in Ireland, planted the seeds of law and order, Henry planted also, however unwittingly, fresh seeds of unending division."

In 1174, de Glanville, with the aid of certain barons of Yorkshire, of which county he had just been made High Sheriff, raised a band of knights, and marched northwards to oppose William the Lion, King of Scotland, the powerful enemy of Henry II., who had invaded the north of England. The High Sheriff surprised the Scottish king, who, feeling himself secure, was amusing himself by tilting in a meadow near Alnwick Castle, and the monarch and his nobles were easily captured on July 12th, the very day that Henry II. was doing his famous penance at the tomb of Thomas à Becket. Sore with the stripes his royal shoulders had received at Canterbury, Henry was in bed when de Glanville's messenger came with the news of the victory,

---

[3] I have ascertained that this signature is in the ablative case, the work of a scribe, and not original.

which the king having joyfully heard, at once ascribed to the favour of the saint.

Promotion for the High Sheriff rapidly followed. In 1176, Ranulph de Glanville was made a Justice of the King's Court, and a Justice Itinerant of the Northern Circuit, and four years afterwards Henry raised him to the exalted position of Chief Justiciary of all England.

Under his direction the King completed his judicial reforms, and "at the instance, it is supposed of Henry II., Glanville wrote, or super-intended the writing of, the *Tractatus de legibus et consuetudinibus regni Angliæ*, which is divided into fourteen books, and is chiefly a practical treatise on the forms of procedure in the *curia regis*, or King's Court . . . As the source of our knowledge regarding the earliest form of the *curia regis*, and for the information it affords regarding ancient customs and laws, it is of great value to the student of English history."[4] De Glanville's treatise is considered of especial value to legal students, as it deals with the old law before the modifications of Magna Charta.

Towards the close of the king's life, on news arriving that Jerusalem had fallen into the hands of the Turks, a new Crusade was determined on, and Baldwin, Archbishop of Canterbury, ac-

[4] *Encyclopædia Britannica.*

companied by Ranulph de Glanville, put on armour and the white cross, and preached the Crusade in Wales. The death of the king, however, delayed the preparations.

The Lord Chief Justice was present and assisted at the Coronation of Richard I. in 1189, when Westminster Abbey was the scene of a gorgeous ceremonial. But the day was marked by a fierce and cruel outburst of the populace against the Jews, numbers of whom, with their wives and children, were brutally murdered. Richard sent Ranulph de Glanville and other officers to quell the outbreak, but they were obliged to fly for their lives, and return to the king, who issued a proclamation, possibly at the instance of the Chief Justice, declaring the Jews to be under the protection of the crown.

Soon after, the king strained every nerve to raise funds for the third Crusade, and on de Glanville resigning his office of Chief Justiciary, Richard put it up for sale, and Hugh Pudsey, Bishop of Durham, was the purchaser. De Glanville then determined to join the Crusade without delay, and accordingly made his way to the Holy Land for the last enterprise of his life. He was present at the Siege of Acre, 1190, during which he fell "fighting valiantly," says Lord Campbell, dying as a Crusader, in what was then esteemed the noblest and most glorious cause. He has been described by a modern writer as " a man of great ability and undoubted probity," a testimony to his virtues which forms a suitable epitaph to the memory of a great, wise, and true man.

Ranulph de Glanville had issue by his wife Barta or Bertha, three daughters, who on his death became his co-heiresses. Maud, the eldest, married William de Auberville; Amabilla married Ranulph de Ardern; Helwisa married Robert filius Robert, and founded Corham Abbey in Yorkshire.

PATRONS OF THE ADVOWSON OF S. MARGARET, UPTON.

Prior and Canons of Butley Priory,
Suffolk ... ... 1171-1538.

LIST OF SOME OF THE PRIORS OF BUTLEY
(CHIEFLY COMPILED FROM NORRIS' MSS.)

Frater Nich. de Wittlesham,
Canon 1307
Fr. Ricard⁰ de Hoxne, Canon 1309
Frat. Will. de Geytone, Canon
and Cellarer 1311
Fr. Alexʳ de Stratford, on death
of Geyton 1332
Frat. Matthew de Pakenham,
on death of Stratford ... 1333

Fr. Alex^r de Drenkeston after
   cession of Pakenham   ... 1353
Fr. John Baxter.
Fr. Will. de Halesworth, after
   cession of Baxter 1374
Fr. Will. Randeworth, Prfectus 1410
Fr. Will. Poley, elected Prior after
   death of Will. Randeworth... 1444
Thomas the Prior, in 1483
Prior Ryvere, in 1505
Robert Bremmore, *circ.* ... 1506
Thomas Manning, alias Sud-
   burn or Sudborne, Bishop of
   Ipswich, last Prior 1538
The Crown, on the Dissolution of Butley
   Priory ... ... *circ.* 1538
The Lady Anne of Cleve ... *circ.* 1540-1557
The Crown ... ... *circ.* 1557-1600
Bishops of Ely (Martin Heton, Bishop of
   Ely, received the advowson on Queen
   Elizabeth taking certain manors in Cam-
   bridgeshire from that See) ... 27th June, 1600
Bishop of Norwich (on an exchange of
   livings with Ely)[5] ... ... 4th June, 1852

---

[5] The patronage of Ranworth with Upton was transferred from the Bishop of Ely to the Bishop of Norwich under order of the Queen in Council, 15th May, 1852, gazetted 4th June, 1852, and taking effect from the last-mentioned date.

VICARS.

DATE OF INSTITUTION.

William the clerk (Add. MS., 8843).

Thome de Wython, Capellanus, admitted
by Bishop William de Raleigh   ... *cir.* 1240

Master Hugo de Upton appears to have been
tenant of the Upton Glebe about this time.

Roger de Jakesle   ...   ...   2 non. Aug., 1304
Still vicar in 1328.

John de Wesenham resigned   1331

Robert de Aylesham, alias Robert de Petra
de Aylsham   ...   ...   4 non. May, 1331

Exchanged with Kirkton. One Robert de
Aylesham was Abbot of S. Benet's in 1349.

John Reignald   ...   ...   xi. kal. May, 1333
Exchanged with Gillingham All Saints.

William de Letton or Leiton   20th Mar., 1347

Exchanged with Bokenham Parva (now
Buckenham Tofts).

Peter Brome or Brom de Burgh   1349

John Smalewood de Beketon   7th Aug., 1361

Ralph de Sythyng ...   ...   10th Oct., 1383

Thomas Smith resigned   1417

William Hawet, alias Spaldyng, presbyter
27th Oct., 1417

On resignation of Thomas Smith. Exchanged with Bewesfeld, Canterbury Diocese.

William Blythe, presbyter ...   2nd Sept., 1418

On resignation of Hawet. Exchanged with
Stanynghale.

Thomas Clerk ... ... 5th Mar., 1433
> On resignation of William Blyth.

John Cappe, presbyter ... 10th Aug., 1440
> On resignation of Thomas Clerk.[6]

Thomas Sabyn, B.A.... ... 29th Dec., 1444

Edward Skoteman, presbyter... 10th Dec., 1450
> On resignation of Thomas Sabyn. The
> Vicar of Upton received 2s. at the funeral of
> John Paston, 1466.—*Paston Letters*, i. 267.

William Kene, LL.B.... ... 25th Jan., 1467
> On death of Edward Skoteman. A feoffee
> for Elizabeth Poynings *née* Paston, 1468.—
> *Paston Letters*, ii. 330.

Robert Framlyngham, resigned 1483

Thomas Gresmer, or Gressemer, priest, 27th Jan., 1483
> On resignation of Robert Framlyngham,
> last vicar.

Alexander Todde ... ... 25th June, 1511

John Thuxton, or Thruxton ... 12th Nov., 1515

Dominus Thomas Bungay, alias Thrower,
Canonicus ... ... 17th June, 1517
> On resignation of John Thuxton, last vicar.

Dominus John Hexham, Capellanus, 27th Mar., 1529
> On death of Thomas Thrower.

George Waryng, Capellanus ... 21st Jan., 1530
> On death of John Hexham.

William Moresone, Capellanus 12th Mar., 1533
> On resignation of George Waryng.

---

[6] Thomas Clerk, "Chaplain of Upton," died 1444, and was buried in the chancel of Upton Church. Vide extract from his will, Chapter VII.

Dominus Christopher Sands, presbyter,

26th May, 1550

> On death of William Moresone. "Pre-
> sented by Anne de Cleve, daughter of John,
> late Duke of Cleve, and sister of William,
> now Duke of Cleve."—Institution Book.

John Fitche, presbyter   ...   20th June, 1556

> Bishop of Norwich, by lapse.

Robert Hacon, Hackon, or Hakyn, 26th Sept., 1558

> "Vicker here and pson of fysshelie."—
> Parish Register.

Matthew Ode...   ...   ...   15th July, 1559

> On death of Hacon. Also Rector of Fishley.

Edward Hiltoune   ...   ...   22nd Sept., 1568

Thomas Deyrton, probably about   1575

> He was instituted to Fishley, 11th Nov.,
> 1577; but I can find no record of his in-
> stitution to Upton in the Institution Books.
> 1618, "Thomas Deyrton, Clarke, was buried
> the 4 daye of Aprill."—Register. Lessees of
> rectorial glebe and tithe: 1600, Robert
> Bensley;[7] 1615, William Harborne and
> Elizabeth Daynes.

Thomas More (on death of Deyrton)   ...   1618

> Rector of Fishley, 2nd May, 1618. Or-
> dained 7th June, 1612. Died July, 1647, and
> buried at Fishley.

Berney Shepherd   ...   ...   10th Aug., 1647

> "Vicar of Upton and person of fyshlie."—
> Parish Register. Buried at Fishley, Feb.
> 22nd, 1657, only thirteen days after his wife
> Bridget was buried at Fishley Church.

[7] *Add. MS.*, 5847, p. 117, Brit. Mus.

John More, the Commonwealth "Vicar of
Upton" ... ... *circ.* 1659

> He signs himself "Vicar of Upton" in the
> Parish Register.

Robert Goodwyn, M.A. ... 17th Dec., 1661

> Instituted by Edward, Bishop of Norwich,
> on the presentation of Matthew, Bishop of
> Ely. Ordained priest by Henry, Bishop of
> Chichester. Instituted to Fishley, 17th July,
> 1672. Buried Feb. 12th, 1678. Matilda his
> wife, buried at Fishley, 25th March, 1673.

[John Forbie,[8] Clerk, A.M., presented by
Peter, Bishop of Ely, 28th Mar., 1679, but
probably not inducted.]

Samuel Style, M.A. ... ... 19th June, 1679

> Rector of Fishley, 1st April, 1679.

Jonathan Newhouse, B.A. ... ... *circ.* 1690

> Rector of Fishley, 24th July, 1690. He
> appears to have been subsequently Rector of
> Boyton, and died about 1721.

Henry Nelson, A.M. ... ... 30th Nov., 1698

> Also Vicar of Ranworth (*Add. MS.* 5847,
> Brit. Mus.) Rector of Fishley, 23rd May,
> 1722. Buried Nov. 4th, 1723.

William Mackay, A.M. ... 10th Jan., 172$\frac{3}{4}$

> On death of last Incumbent, Rector of
> Fishley. Vicar of Ranworth from 1722 to
> 1725. Vicar of Runham.

---

[8] *Add. MS.*, 5847, p. 117, Brit. Mus.

D

Thomas Dod, A.M. ...   ...   28th Oct., 1752
> On death of Mackay. He appears to have been Curate of Acle, 1733. Rector of Billockby from 1730. On his institution to Upton the two benefices were united for his life.

John Dennison   ...   ...   6th April, 1775
> On death of Thomas Dod. Curate of Hemblington. Became Vicar of Loddon and Rector of Hautbois, 1790.

Charles Gogill, became Vicar on consolidation of Upton with Ranworth, 26th Feb., 1790
> Vicar of Ranworth, 1771.

Francis Edward Say ...   ...   13th Dec., 1793
> And Vicar of Ranworth.

Ven. John Oldershaw, B.D. ...   2nd Mar., 1795
> On cession of Say.

John William Greaves   ...   20th April, 1843
> On death of Archdeacon Oldershaw. Vicar of Ranworth. Last presentation by Bishop of Ely. Ordained in Diocese of Ely. Buried at Ranworth, April, 1886.

Percival Oakley Hill ...   ...   28th May, 1886
> Ordained in Diocese of Norwich, Deacon, Trinity, 1881 ; Priest, Trinity, 1882.

CURATES.

William Beevor	...	...	...	... 1701
Timothy Jones	...	...	...	... 1723
John Thomas Suckling	...	...	...	... 1795

James Carlos   1795
James B. Thompson ...   licensed 25th Nov., 1799
J. Gilbert   1800
Charles Boutell   1803
Thomas Marshall   ..   licensed 16th Dec., 1804
Robert Steele ...   ...   licensed 21st Apr., 1807
John Athow ...   ...   licensed 7th Jan., 1814
John Leeds ...   ...   licensed 31st Mar., 1814
John Hammond Fiske   licensed 9th June, 1816
John Beevor Berney, A.B.   licensed 20th July, 1817
William Taylor Worship, licensed 22nd Sept., 1822
Vicar of Stokesby.
Thomas Corbould   ...   licensed 4th Nov., 1826
In 1858 Rector of Tacolneston.
Philip Utten Brown, B.A.   licensed 5th July, 1837
Smith Churchill, B.A.   licensed 27th July, 1840
Afterwards Rector of Boughton.
John Henry Wise   1843
Afterwards Rector of Brendon, Devon, and
Rural Dean.
William Horsley Barr Hamilton   10th Mar., 1881
Percival Oakley Hill...   1883
Presented to the Vicarage, 1886.

NOTES ON LIST OF VICARS.

The entry of burial of Robert Hacon, Vicar, is given in the Register under date 1558, as follows :

"S\ Robert Hacon vicker here and pson of fysshlee the vi^th of December."

The title of Sir is also prefixed to the name of Thomas Deyrton in the Register under date 1577.

In reference to this title, the Rev. Edward Marshall, in his *Woodstock Manor*, writes : "It was assigned to the clergy at an early period. As to the application of the term to the clergy, Fuller observes in his *History of Abbeys* : 'Such priests as have the addition of 'Sir' before their Christian names were men not graduated at the Universities, being in orders, but not in degrees.' He has been censured for this remark. But he is so far supported by a list of certain chantries in St. Paul's Cathedral which he inserts, that the two priests who have the title of 'Mr.' and not of 'Sir,' are also the only two who are described as 'graduates.'"

Mr. Marshall further points out that "Sir," being the English equivalent of "Dominus," was the academical title applied to Bachelors of Arts, who were not considered in those days to possess a full degree, the B.A. being but a stepping-stone to the full graduate rank of M.A., which latter carried with it the title " Mr."

"Sir" Thomas Deyrton, one of the Elizabethan Vicars, had a long tenure of office, during part of which time he appears to have had an unpleasant experience of the "aggrieved parishioner," for we find him "named" in the Archdeacon's Court on one or two occasions, videlicet—

"1586. Thomas Dierton notat^r for abusing his parishioners with evil words. He teacheth not the catechisme as he is comanded to the youth."

"Mr Thomas Dierton n^r (notatur) that he necligentlie supplieth his duetie not reading of devine service, viz., uppon the nynth daie of October he redd not divine service by hymself nor provided any person to read devine service, but the clark of the parish did supplie his place and so red some part of service both forenone and after none being a mere laie mann . . . . 1597."

But the "necligent" Vicar discovered a worse form of "necligence" in some of his parishioners, for at the same visitation he appears to have "named" Robert Tailor, "that the same thrashed corne on divers saboth daies within this halfe yeare last past, quarto die mensis Aprilis, 1596;" and William Sybell, "for working and going to cart on the Saboth, xix September, 1597." It is added "This (these) persons fee owing for not going the pambulacon (perambulation) about the circuite of their parrish in the rogaćon week, according to the quenenes Iniunctions in this yeare 1597." [9]

Fourteen years after this we find the Vicar

[9] Records preserved in the Registry of the Archdeaconry of Norwich.

faithfully performing his duty in Upton Church, when a case of brawling took place, which was made the subject of a presentment in the Archdeacon's Court held in Acle Church in 1612, as follows: "William Enderton, comonly called by the name of Wicked Will, servant of Robert ffisher, and Symon Bullock of the said towne, did profanely and disorderlie behave themselves in this sort, viz., uppon Christmas daie last in the tyme of evening praier they came into the parrish church of Upton aforesaid, with a great whalles bone uppon their shoulders, and wth ys birds, a robin redbrest and a wrenne, tied by a thrid and hanging uppon the said bone, the said Wittm making a great and a roring noyse all waie of his coming, and they went staggering and reeling too and fro in the midd allie in a scoffing and a wild profane manner, by the minister's seate (the sayd minister being reading devine service) they fell downe as thoughe they were hevely or grevously loaden, and then and there the said Wicked Will in such wild and p̃fane and lewde manner as befor, kneling uppon his knees he praid for the sayd Mr. Deyrton and his wife and for his great dog (to) the dishonoᵣ of almightie god, p̃fanaõn of the place, and evill example of others. Sexto Aprilis, 1612." He appears to have been ordered to acknowledge his fault in the face of the church, a far milder punish-

ment than would have been meted out to him
under the Brawling Act in the present day. It
is probable that the "great whalles bone" was
preserved in the church as a memento of the
occurrence, for a large bone, measuring 5 ft. 4 ins.
in length, formerly kept in the belfry, and now
preserved at the Vicarage, may well have been
the identical bone put to so profane a use by
"Wicked Will" and his companion.

Respecting an Ancient Pension.

A pension of xxxs. per annum was payable to
the Vicars of Upton by the Priors of Butley.
The first record of it appears to be a note from
the Charter of the Prior of Butley, fol. 47, quoted
in *Add. MS.* 8843, Brit. Mus.

"And the Vicar of Vpton had a pention of
xxx shill. p annū payable by the prior of Butley
by the confirmation of John of Oxford, bishop."

This confirmation of Bishop John of Oxford
must have been 1175—1200, and the pension, no
doubt, was settled on the Vicar at the founding of
Upton Church.

In 1615, Thomas Deyrton, Vicar, brought an
action against the lessees of the Rectory, in the
Court of Exchequer, the record of which is

preserved in the Public Record Office, and is as
follows :—

"Jacobus Dei grā Anglie Scotie Franc et Hiƀnie
Rex, fidei Defens, &c. Diltis nobis Jacobo Scambler Arᵒ, Johi Smythe Arᵒ, Ricō Jenkinson Arᵒ, &
Johi Holte sacre theologie bachalario Saltm Sciatis
q̃d nos de fidelitaƫ industr & pvidis circū speccoibȝ
vr̃is in negotiis nr̃is agend pluriūm confiden
assignaviɱ vos ac vobis quatuor tribȝ & duobȝ
vr̃m plenam p̃tatem & aūctatem damus & com-
mittiɱ p p̃ntes ad testes quoscūɋ de & sup
quibusdam articlis sive interrogaƭ tm̃ ex pte Thome
Dierton clici quer̃ qm̃ ex pte Wiⱦmi Harborne
arⁱ & Elizabeth Daynes vid. defend. coram vobis
aut tribȝ siue duobȝ vr̃m exhibend siue deliƀand
diligenter exãiand Et ideo vobis mandamus qd ad
hm̃oi diem & locū suie dies et loca quos vel que
ad hoc pvideritis aut tres siue duo vr̃m pvid̃inƫ
testes p̃dcos coram vobis aut tribȝ siue duobȝ vr̃m
veniri faciatis & evocetis ac ip̃os testes & eorƫ
quemlt p se sepatim de & sup articlis siue interr
p̃d sup sacra sua coram vobis aut tribȝ siue duobȝ
vr̃m p sc̃a Dei evangel corporalr p̃stand diligenter
exãietis aut tres siue duo vrm̃ exãient exaiac̃õesɋ
suas recipiatis & in scriptis in pgameno redigatis
Et eas cū sic cepitis aut tres siue duo vrm̃ cepint
Baronibȝ de Sccīo nr̃o apud Westm. in octav. sci
Martini px. futur̃ sub sigillis vr̃is aut triū siue

duorꝰ vr̃m claus. mittatis aut tres siue duo vr̃m mittant unacū interrogat ꝑd & hoc brē proviso semꝑ qd ꝑd defend. hẽant ꝑmonicõem ꝑ spaciū xiiij dierꝰ de die & loco primo sessionis vr̃e suꝑ hoc bre ante execucõem eiusdem. T. Laurencio Tanfeld mil. apud Westm. quarto die Octob. anno R. n. anglie Franc & Hiber xiii° & Scotie xlix°."

Interrogatories to be ministered to the Witnesses to be produced on part of Thomas Dyerton, Clerk, and on part of William Harborne and Elizabeth Daynes.

1. Do you know the parties to the suit, and for how long have you known them?

2. Do you know, of your own knowledge, or have you seen any records whereby it doth appear that the parsonage of Upton, in the county of Norfolk, was parcell of the possessions of the late dissolved Monastery or Priory of Butlie in the county of Suffolk?

3. Do you know or have you heard of any pension to be issuing and going out of the said rectory and parsonage of Upton, and payable unto the vicar of Upton for the time being, and what was the said pension which was yearly due and payable to the said vicar?

4. Do you know of any leases heretofore made by Kings and Queens of this Realm of the said parsonage, and have not the said lessees paid a yearly pension to the vicar of Upton for the time being?

5. Have you not known or credibly heard that the said farmors and lessees of the said parsonage of Upton have been allowed a certain sum of money upon the payment of their rent in respect of the pencon due to the said vicar for the time being?

6. Have not the said Elizabeth Daynes and the said William Harborne, or those under whom they claim, had an interest and estate of and in the said parsonage of Upton for many years past, and for how long tyme?

7. What other matter or thing do you know touching the pencon of twenty shillings a yere issuing out of the said parsonage of Upton to the vicar there? Declare the trueth herein.

Depositions of divers Witnesses produced.

Edward Hilton of Lingwood, Norfolk, clerk, aged 74 years, or thereabouts :—

1. Had known complt. and Elizabeth Daynes for 40 years, and Wm. Harborne for 20 years.

2. Hath heard y^t ye parsonage of Upton was parcell of ye late priory of Butley.

3. Hath heard there hath been a yearly pencon going out of the said parsonage to the vicar there, but what he cannot depose.

4. Hath heard that leases have been made of ye parsonage by ye late Queen Elizabeth, but whether the lessees paid any pension to ye vicar of Upton he cannot say.

5. He cannot depose.

6. Hath heard y^t ye def^ts have had estates in the said parsonage of Upton, but for how many years he knoweth not.

7. Further he cannot depose.

William Taylor of Upton, carpenter, aged 71 years :—

1. Hath known comp^t and Elizabeth Daynes for forty years, and William Harborne for 20 years.

2. Hath heard y^t ye parsonage of Upton was parcel of Butley Priory possessions.

3. Hath heard from divers old men of Upton that there was a pencon of twenty shillings payable to the vicar for the time being out of the rectory.

4, 5, 6, and 7. He cannot depose further.

Messrs. Scambler and Holt executed and endorsed the warrant. They held their enquiry at Ludham on 13th Nov., 1615.

"Decrees and Orders (Exchequer),

"14 James, vol. 23, fol. 112.

"Die Lune xxix° die Aprilis xiiii° Jac.

"Upon openeinge of the matter dependinge in this Courte by Englishe Bill betweene Thomas Dyerton, Clerke, plaintiff, and William Harborne and Elizabeth Daynes, Defendants—It is Ordered by the courte that the said Defendants shall be dismissed this Courte without costs.

"Babb p P.

"West p Def."

The Vicar won the case, and his successors reap the benefit of his vigorous action. The pension is still paid out of the Great Tithe (by the Ecclesiastical Commissioners), and in modern value it amounts to 6d. per diem or £9. 2s. 6d. per annum.

Two vicars besides Mr. Dyerton had a long tenure of office, viz., the Rev. J. W. Greaves, forty-three years, and the Ven. Archdeacon Oldershaw, forty-eight years. The latter was a typical pluralist, as is shewn by the following licence of non-residence preserved amongst the parish records: "We, Charles, Bishop of Norwich, hereby license you, John Oldershaw, Clerk, Rector of Redenhall with the chapel of Harleston, Vicar of Ranworth with Upton annexed, and Vicar of

Ludham, in the County of Norfolk and our Diocese of Norwich, to be absent from your benefice of Ranworth with Upton annexed aforesaid for two years from the date hereof on account of y⁰ Parsonage House belonging to your said Benefice of Ranworth with Upton being unfit for y⁰ residence of yourself and family : such unfitness not being occasioned by your own negligence, and such house being kept in such repair as shall be satisfactory to us and our successors. You residing at Starston, and performing the duties of your said parish of Harleston. Given under our hand, this twenty-eighth day of February in the year of our Lord one thousand eight hundred and four, and in the twelfth year of our consecration.

" C. Norwich."

Upton was consolidated with Ranworth, Feb. 26th, 1790, as appears by the " Diocesan Book," when the Rev. Charles Gogill, Vicar of Ranworth, became Vicar of the united parishes, but the Institution Books do not apparently give any record of his institution to Upton. The two parishes were disunited by Order in Council, 3rd March, 1873, which took effect on the next voidance. A previous union of these benefices occurred in 1698.

The *Ordination Book*, vol. i., gives the following

particulars of ordination candidates, who subsequently became Vicars of Upton :—

"1682. Henry Nelson, of St. John's College in
Cambridge. Borne in Garsdall in y⁰ County of
York, in the 25th year of my age, to be ordained
priest in y⁰ Lᵈ Bishops Chappel in Norwich.

" Hen. Nelson."

" I, Samuel Style, Batchelor of Arts, Corpˢ Xti
Coll. in Cambridge, of 23 years current, born in
the county of Norfolk, in the Parish of St. Peter
in Norwich, to be curate to Mr. Thomas Scamler,
Rector of Drayton cum Marlingford, to be ordained
Deacon in the Cathedral Church in Norwʰ.

" Samuel Style."

" I, Jonathan Newhowse, Batchelor of Arts, of
Gonv. Caii. Coll. in Cambridge, of 23 years current,
born in the County of Norfolke, in the parish of
St. Stephen's in Norwich, to be Curate to Mʳ Wᵐ
plumsted, Rector of Wickmer, to be ordained
Deacon in y⁰ Cathedrall Church in Norwich.

"Jonathan Newhowse."

POSSESSIONS OF THE CHURCH.

Recorded in Add. MS. 8843, fo. 46.

Vpton Eccłia. Norff. Carta Johis prioris super
appropriatione eccliæ Vpton cum aliis in eadem

carta contentis queratur inferius tertio loco sedæ virgæ.

Confirmatio Joħis Ēpi 2di super eadem eccłia nobis confirmat queratur in eodem loco.

Confirmatio Wiłłi de Ralegh Ēpi suꝑ eadem appropaconē et taxatio vicariæ in qua taxatione assignat medietatem octo decem acras terræ quas Mag^r Hugo de Vpton de nobis tenet in eadem villa portione dicti vicar qui ꝑ tempore fuerit.

Carta Walteri de Suffeld Ēpi super prďcis xviij acris totaliter nobis assignat de consensu Thome capellani tunc vicarii iɓm reddendo vicario et successoribus quinque solidos per ann. in festo Sce Margarete.

Confirmatio Symonis prioris & conventus Norwici suꝑ eccła prdcā et taxatione.

Confirmatio Jacobi de Terentino decani de Holt ďni Archidiaconi Norff. ꝑ curatoris sede Norwic vacante & ipso visitante suꝑ eadem eccłiā appriand.

Carta Wiłłi clerici quondam vicarii ecclie přd suꝑ 12 acris terræ quas in vsus ꝑprios retinuimus quando eum ad dc̄am vicarium přsentavimus tenend de nobis ꝑ servitium xx solid ꝑ ann.— Abbreviatio Cartaꝣ prioratus Butley, Suffol., 46, 47.

And the Vicar of Vpton had a pention of xxx shill ꝑ annũ payable by the prior of Butley by the confirmation of John of Oxford, bishop.—Fol. 47.

Carta Wiłłi de Rahalee, Episcopi Norwic, super-admissione Thome de Wython capellani ad vicariam ecclie Vpton ad pŕsentationem prioris Butley et taxatione vicariæ ejusdem ecctie.—Fol. 47b.

And concerning the pension of 30 shill. payable to the Vicar of Vpton by the prior of Butley yearly, see the same book, fol. 47.

[On back of a slip.] The Archbishop of Canterbury's confirmation.—Fol. 48 and 49. The taxation of Upton in the 21st year of King Edward the first was xvi*l.* xiii*s.* iiii*d.*, tenths xxx*l.* iii*s.* iiii*d.*—Blofield Deanery, fol. 53.

———————

Rot. Hund., p. 512. The Bishop of Norwich held land in Upton, as member of his Manor of Blofield.

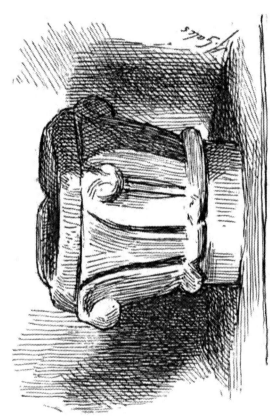

NORMAN PISCINA OF DE GLANVILLE'S CHURCH AT UPTON, DISCOVERED 1885.

From a Pen and Ink Sketch by Mr. Henry Gales.

CHAPTER III.

Of the Church: its Re-building, Lady and Becket Chapels, Rood-screen, Ancient Lights, Guilds, Font, Bells, Communion Plate, Inventory of Church Goods, and Restoration.

FOR about two centuries the Norman church of Ranulph de Glanville was the spiritual home of the people of Upton. How it ceased to exist can only be matter for speculation— possibly lightning, or some accidental fire may have destroyed it. That it was superseded by the present fabric in the Perpendicular period is shewn from the fact that much of the Norman stonework was utilized in the existing structure. The Norman piscina was discovered in the restoration of 1885, built into the wall of the north aisle above one of the windows. It is now affixed for security in the

stoup near the south door, which was also brought
to light during the restoration of the church.
Other fragments of Norman work were found,
some of which are preserved in the vestry. With
the exception, perhaps, of the tower, the present
church cannot have been commenced before 1380,
and was probably not completed till the fifteenth
century. The ten windows of the aisles exhibit
a transom in the tracery, and are quoted in the
British Archæological Journal for 1890 as specimens of "fully-developed Perpendicular." I have
been unable to trace the re-building of the church
to any particular person, and it is probable that
this work was carried out by the Prior and Canons
of Butley.

The proportions of the church are fine, and
altogether present a strikingly beautiful appearance.

Cubic space, about	...	110,000 cub. ft.
Length of chancel	... ...	40 ft. 5 in.
Breadth of chancel	... ...	19 ft.
Length of nave ...	... ...	68 ft. 8 in.
Breadth of nave ...	... ...	20 ft. 4 in.
Height of nave ...	... ...	40 ft.
Length of north aisle	... ...	64 ft. 6 in.
Breadth of north aisle	... ...	12 ft. 1 in.
Length of south aisle	... ...	64 ft.
Breadth of south aisle	... ...	12 ft. 1 in.

It will be seen that the extreme length of the
church (without the tower) is 109 ft., and its
breadth 44 ft. 6 in.

PISCINA AND REMAINS OF CONSECRATION CROSS,

LADY CHAPEL, UPTON CHURCH.

FROM A DRAWING BY MR. HENRY GALES.

The windows are well preserved, and good specimens of Perpendicular work. The large east window of the chancel is especially fine, and the twelve lights in its tracery were evidently designed for figures of the Twelve Apostles in painted glass. Some fragments of ancient stained glass are preserved in the east windows of the aisles.

Beneath these windows were altars in pre-Reformation times. Their piscinas still remain, that in the south aisle being in excellent preservation, with a charming bit of flamboyant tracery at the top, and the remains of a consecration cross in close proximity.

This east end of the south aisle formed the Lady Chapel,[1] and that of the north aisle, I take it, was the Chapel of S. Thomas à Becket.[2]

---

[1] "My body to be buryed befor the pyktur of our lady in the south ysle of the Chirche of Seynt Margrette, virgyn & martyr, of Upton forseyd."—Will of Thos. Andrews, 1488.

[2] "To be buried in the Church of St. Margaret before the high altar of the blessed Thomas the Martyr."—Will of Thomas Wycete, 1467.

The Norman church was founded the year after the murder of Thomas à Becket, Archbishop of Canterbury, Tuesday, December 29th, 1170. The leading position in the State held by our Founder must have brought him into close relationship with Becket, whose memory De Glanville may well have desired to perpetuate in his new foundation at Upton, as soon as the Archbishop was canonized. A full-length painting of S. Thomas the Martyr in vestments occurs on the Ranworth Screen, and a fresco of his murder is to be seen on the south wall of the chancel of South Burlingham Church.

THE ROOD-SCREEN.

The base of the ancient Rood-screen remains beneath the lofty chancel arch, and is in excellent preservation, the rood-loft and "dore[3]" having disappeared, unless, indeed, the "dore" was merely the open entrance to the chancel. On the north side are four panels under gilded bosses in relief, containing paintings of the four Latin Fathers, each about 2 ft. 8 in. in height, SS. Augustin, Jerome, Gregory the Great, and Ambrose. They are thus described by L'Estrange in his MS. dated 1870, in the possession of Mr. Walter Rye, to whom I am indebted for a copy.

1. *St. Augustin.* "A Bishop in red cope, green mitre, book in right hand, crook in left turned inwards."

2. *St. Jerome.* "A Cardinal, red hat, green cloak, with slits for arms, red book."

3. *St. Gregory the Great.* "A Pope, triple crown, red cope, amice, open book."

4. *St. Ambrose.* "An Archbishop, red mitre, albe with apparel, red dalmatic, green chasuble, pall, crook in right hand, book in left."

---

[3] The screen door is referred to in the will of Agnes Wynn, whose memorial brass is still *in situ*, "to be buried in Church of St. Margaret in the middle aley before the chancel dore."

PANEL OF ROODSCREEN, REPRESENTING S. AMBROSE, UPTON CHURCH.

FROM A PEN AND INK SKETCH BY MR. HENRY GALES.

On the south side are the painted figures of four female saints on oak panels.

1. "*St. Helen*, crowned, veiled, robed in ermine, with the cross of our Lord's Passion in her right hand, a black book in her left."

2. "*St. Etheldreda*, wimple, pastoral staff, red book."

3. *St. Joanna, Queen of Spain*, "veiled, red mantle, bowl in right hand, frail basket in left hand with loaves in it."

4. "*St. Agatha.* A virgin with long hair holding a breast with pincers by the nipple."

Above, on the transom, is :—

" . . . . llyā Wynne and Anneys ys wyfe et cetera."

Husenbeth, in his *Emblems of Saints*, notes SS. Etheldreda and Joanna as occuring with their emblems on the " Rood-screen, Upton, Norfolk."

The date of the canonization of St. Joanna, 1505, coupled with the remains of the inscription, make it probable that the screen was re-painted subsequently to the death of Anneys or Agnes Wynne in 1506, at all events on the south side. [Extracts from the wills of William and Agnes Wynne are given in Chapter VII.] The screen itself, probably, dates from forty or fifty years earlier. To the north and south of the chancel arch, and near the screen, are two consecration crosses, fairly well preserved, brought to light in 1885.

LIGHTS AND GUILDS.

The following Lights were in the church, viz., those of St. Margaret, Blessed Virgin Mary, St. John Baptist, and St. Nicholas.

Of the last named saint there was formerly a "tabernacle" containing an image of St. Nicholas. There is reason to believe that this was affixed to the half pillar at the east end of the north aisle, close to the present pulpit. Before it is the brass of Thomas Wesyt, who died in 1513. The remains of fresco work may be traced, and an iron staple still remaining, about 9 ft. 9 in. from the floor, may well have supported the "tabernacle."[4]

THE GUILDS

in connection with the church were

    1.   The Guild of S. Margaret, the Patron Saint.
    2.   „   „   the Blessed Virgin Mary.

[4] "Repair of the image and tabernacle of St. Nicholas, Bishop, in same church, 40s."—Will of Nicholas Cossey, 1479.

"To paynting and gilding of the tabernacle of St. Nicholas in the same church, 6s. 8d."—Will of William Wynne, 1505.

3. The Guild of S. John Baptist.

4. „ „ S. Peter.

That there was not always, in those days, zeal enough to maintain the work of a Church Guild, may be inferred from the will of William Wynne, 1505 : "to the guild of St. Peter 6s. 8d. on condition that the brethren and sistern will begin the guild and uphold it."

THE FONT

is remarkably fine and in very fair preservation, although some of the figures have been sadly mutilated. It is a beautiful specimen of early English work. Three large octagonal steps form a striking approach to the font; the top step is divided from the second by open quatrefoils, and supported at intervals by dogs in sitting postures.

A finely-carved pedestal rises from a circle of foliage and queer-looking animals—two lions joined by their tails, two dogs united by their heads, and a monster having one head and two bodies. Standing out in relief upon this pedestal are figures under exquisite canopies and representing the two Sacraments, to wit:—*Holy Communion*, a bishop in vestments, holding pastoral staff in right hand, supported to right and left by angels bearing each a candlestick;

next a priest holding an open missal; then a
second priest with the elements. Both the latter
wear the dalmatic, maniple, and stole. *Holy
Baptism* is signified by three sponsors, one male
and two female, one of the latter with an infant
in her arms in curious swaddling clothes, the
others with rosaries: all wearing the lay dress
of the period.

The very handsome bowl of the font is described
in *L'Estrange's MSS.*, vol. ix.:—

			Emblems of
"On the E. panel of bowl ...	...	St. John Ev.
„	N.	„	... ...	St. Matthew.
„	W.	„	... ...	St. Luke.
„	S.	„	... ...	St. Mark.

Intermediate panels:—Angels, north-east and
south-west, holding shields; south-east, a guitar;
north-west, cymbals. The bowl is supported by
eight half angels holding crowths, books, shields,
&c."

The font was originally painted, as denoted by
small fragments of the ancient colouring still
remaining.

The west arch of the church is filled up with
masonry, a work probably found necessary when
the tower fell. In this masonry the stone outline
of a window was brought to light in 1885, and

the brickwork was removed which blocked it up. Above the arch was found [5] the gable line of the old roof of the church, indicating possibly that the clerestory with its eight windows, was built at a later date than the lower part of the church. From a comparison of the flintwork at the top of the ruined tower with that of the clerestory it is probable that the former was raised in height at this later date.

THE BELLS.

There were four bells in the reign of Edward VI., weighing respectively 5, 7, 10, and 14 cwt. A fifth bell remained in its place over the chancel as late as 1725, recorded in a terrier of that date. This would, of course, be the *sanctus* or *saunce* bell. It may have been sold in 1727, although I have found no special faculty authorizing its sale.

" In 1727, a faculty was granted for the sale of three split bells which had stood behind the church door beyond the memory of any man then living." —L'Estrange's *Bells*, p. 229. This faculty is given in the Faculty Book in the Bishop's Office.

" *Upton*, 27 March, 1727. To Wm. Mackey, vicar, Robert Goote and John Norton, church-

---

[5] A line marking this ancient gable has been traced in the new plaster.

wardens, and to Mr. James Jay, one of the chief inhabitants—to sell three split bells standing behind the door, ' £200 having been expended about the church, and yet now not a seat in it but is decayed.' "

These bells may well have been split in the fall of the tower, which *may* have taken place before the sixth year of Edward VI. (1552-3), for the Inventory of Church Goods of that year mentions the existence of the four bells, but assigns one only for the use of Divine Service. That the tower was dilapidated long before 1602 is evident from the following certificate returned to Bishop Redman in that year, quoted in *The East Anglian*, vol. ii. p. 232 :—"Vpton. The Steple there ruynated through the default and necligence of the prishiñrs there long since. The church otherwise is sufficientlie repaired and decentlye kept."[6]

The tower was presumably standing in 1546, when John Poddes of Fishley left 6s. 8d. "to repair of Upton steeple."

The bell still remaining is doubtless the one left by King Edward's Commissioners for use in "devyne service," and "wayen xᶜ." It was cast by one of the Brasyers, the famous Norwich bell

[6] In 1587, Richard Taylor, yeoman, bequeathed "£4 of good English money towards the buildinge uppe of the steple againe, to be paid when the parishioners doe builde upp the same."

founders, probably about 1440, and bears the name
of *Gabriel*, in the following inscription :—

𝕳𝖆𝖈 𝕴𝖓 𝕮𝖔𝖓𝖈𝖑𝖆𝖚𝖊 𝕲𝖆𝖇𝖗𝖎𝖊𝖑 𝕹𝖚𝖈 𝕻𝖆𝖓𝖌𝖊 𝕾𝖚𝖆𝖇𝖊.

Cotman, in his *Architectural Remains* (vol. ii.
pl. 41), gives an etching of the east end of Upton
Church in 1815, with a sketch of the quaint old
bell-house, or shed, under the east window. Here
it had hung for many years, and was swung by its
stay, the foot of the ringer being placed upon the
bell, when required for service. An erection was
made in the shell of the ruined tower in 1867,
where the bell was then hung. The following
inscription is borne on a stone outside the tower :—

This Bell was for upwards
Of two centuries hung in a shed
At the east end of the Church
But removed to its present position
A.D. 1867.

Robert Capon, } Churchwardens.
James B. Parker, }

COMMUNION PLATE.

The pre-Reformation chalices enumerated in the
Inventory of Church Goods of Edw. VI. have, alas!
disappeared. The "chalys," weighing 11½ ozs., left

by King Edward's Commissioners for use " in
the admynystracion of the devyne service" was
replaced in or about the year 1567-8 by a cup of
silver gilt, with large bowl, supported by a stem
resting on a figured pediment. The bowl bears
the legend, on a gilt band,—

✠ THIS CVP IS FOR VPTVN.

The cup bears the Norwich mark, and possesses a
moveable cover of silver (silversmith's mark almost
obliterated), which does duty for a paten. This cup
is still in use. The flagon is of pewter, and appears
to date from William III.

INVENTORY OF CHURCH GOODS, EDWARD VI.

HUNDREDS OF BLOFIELD AND WALSHAM.

Vpton. This inventorie indentid made yᵉ last
day of August in the sixt yere of yᵉ reyne of oʳ
Soṽraigne lord Edward the six by the grace of God
Kyng of Ynglond, Fraunce, and Irelond, Defender
of the feith and in earth of yᵉ churche of Ynglond
the supreme hed, betweyn Willᵐ Fermor, John
Robsart, Xpofer Heydon Knyght, Osbert Mounde-
fore, Robert Berney and John Callybutt, Esquiers,

Comyssioners amongst others assigned by v̄tue of
the Kyng's Maties Comyssion to them directid for
ye survey of Churche goods in the Countie of Norff:
of thon pty, and John Ramsey, Edmund Tayllor,
Willm Gymyngham, Robt Wyn and Robt Gootte
of the forseid town of Vpton of the other ptye,
Wyttenesith y^t there remayneth ĩn the hands and
custodie of the said John Ramsey, Edmund Tayllor,
Willm Gymyngham, Robt Wyn and Robt Gootte
y^e day and yere abovewreten all theis goods and
ornaments here underwreten—

Imp^imis—one chalys w^t y^e patent of
  silver dubbyl gylt conteyning xi
  ounces & di, every ounce iii_s._ x_d._ ...   xlii_s._ ii_d._
Itm—a nother chalys w^t y^e patent
  psell gylt conteyning xiiii ounces
  iii qrs at iii_s._ viii_d._ y^e ounce ...   liiii_s._ i_d._
Itm—a pax of sylver psell gylt con-
  taining ii ounces iii q̃rs ... ...   x_s._ i_d._
Itm—j vestement of blewe velvet w^t
  decon and subdecon ... ...   xl_s._
Itm—j cobe of blewe velvet xx_s._ & j
  of whyte damask x_s._ ... ...   xxx_s._
Itm—j vestement of whyte damask...   iii_s._ iiii_d._
Itm—ii kopys of grene sylck v_s._, j
  vestement of grene silk iii_s._ iiii_d._...   viii_s._ iiii_d_
Itm—j canapie xiii_s._ iiii_d._, and j fruntell
  of grene sylck iii_s._ iiii_d._ ... ...   xvi_s._ viii_d._

Itm—ii ault clothez of whytte sylck...   iii*s.* iiii*d.*

Itm—a sutte of rede sylck ...   ...   v*s.*

Itm—a vestem*t* of black wursted   ...   iii*s.*

Itm—a carde cloth of sylck...   ...   xii*d.*

Itm—a sengyll vestm*t*   ...   ...   xii*d.*

Itm—j kope of blewe velvet   ...   v*s.*

Itm—iiij*or* stepill bells weyinge xxxvi*e*

   whereof the first cont. v*e*, the second

   vii*e*, the iii*d* x*e*, the iiii xiiii*e*   ... xxvii*l.*

Item for brase and

   latten sold in a°

   i & ii E vi*tt* ...   xxv*s.*   Thys

Item for plate and   lix*s.* x*d.* ob.

   other ornam*e*ts   ys   agreed

   sold in a° xxxviii*to*   *p* answer.

   H. Oct...   ...   xxxiiii*s.* x*d.* ob.

The canapie is in thands of Roger Rookewood, who denyeth to deliv*r* the same to the church-wardens.

Roger Rocwood ys contented to answ*r* y*t* or the valewe.[7]

Whereof ys assigned and left to be occupied and vsed in the admynystracion of the devyne service there

The Chalys conteyning xi ounces di & on bell wayen x*e*.

---

[7] In another handwriting and ink.

In wyttenes whereof the seid Comyssion[rs] and other seid psons to theise Inventoriez aĺtnatly have putte theire hands y[e] day and yere above wreten.

p me John Rāsey,
p me Johne Broughton.

THE RESTORATION OF THE CHURCH.

The church having fallen into deplorable dilapidation, it became necessary that a thorough restoration should be effected. The work was commenced by the Ecclesiastical Commissioners in 1879, by the substantial repair of the fabric of the chancel, and the substitution of an oak "wagon" roof for the old one. A heavy beam having fallen in the body of the church in 1875, the congregation migrated to the chancel, and for ten years the nave and aisles were not used for divine service. In 1884 a Committee was appointed at a meeting of parishioners held in the school-room, for the purpose of collecting subscriptions and carrying out the work of restoration. Of this committee the present Vicar was hon. sec., and the Rural Dean, the Rev. Canon Patteson, Rector of Thorpe, became the active chairman, presiding over all the meetings

F

until the committee closed its labours in 1889. In 1885 the fabric of the nave and aisles was thoroughly restored, under the able supervision of Mr. A. S. Hewitt, A.R.I.B.A., of Great Yarmouth, the work being executed by Mr. Evans of South Walsham, builder and contractor. New roofs were found to be absolutely necessary. Some of the best oak grown in the neighbourhood was used for the nave roof, and the massive tie-beams were carefully restored and replaced. The aisles are roofed with the best pitch-pine. The restoration of the stonework of windows and pillars was well carried out by Messrs. Utting of Acle.

In July of the same year the church was re-opened by the Lord Bishop of the Diocese, assisted by the Bishop of Victoria, the Rural Dean, and other clergy, in the presence of a large congregation. The Rev. Canon Patteson preached at the evening service. The offertories for the day amounted to the handsome sum of £87.

In 1888 a further work was carried out in the thorough repair of the porch, and the re-seating the nave with open benches of pitch-pine, a number of the ancient poppy-heads being used with good effect at the east and west ends of the seating, and in the north and south aisles where wood block floors have been laid. Book boards,· with portions of the old oak carving, have also been erected.

The total cost of the restoration, including that of the chancel, carried out by the Ecclesiastical Commissioners, exceeded £2000.[8] It may be added that, in 1885, the Ecclesiastical Commissioners erected handsome oak choir seats, laid a floor of Minton tiles in the chancel, and gave a new communion rail, with brass pillars.

The new pulpit of Corsham stone, bearing four tracery panels with ecclesiastical designs, was erected in 1888 by the present vicar, to the memory of his father, the late Rev. John Oakley Hill, M.A., Rector of Little Rollright, Oxon. At a special re-opening service held on November 15th, 1888, upon the completion of the work of restoration, the Lord Bishop of Norwich, before commencing the sermon, solemnly dedicated the pulpit to the service of Almighty God.

The old Tudor pulpit is preserved as a relic in the Lady Chapel. Previous to the restoration of the church it formed part of a "three-decker" to the south of the chancel arch. Reference is made to it in an entry in the Parish Register, vol. ii., at p. 68.

---

[8] Towards this sum, the Lord Bishop of the Diocese, Miss Edwards of Hardingham, and Canon Patteson, were munificent contributors.

" Memorandum. The Rev. Mr. Mackay, Vicar
of this Parish of Upton, Built a Seate opposite
to the Pulpit and Reading Desk at his own Cost
and Charges wth Chancellor Tanners leave, for
himself and his ffamilys Use, which he the said
William Mackay dedicates to all the Ministers
and their ffamilys Use for ever, desiring that the
afores^{d} Seat may be kept up and maintained by
them at their own proper charges. As witness
my hand this ffirst Day of May, 1739.

"William Mackay, A.M.
"and Vicar of Upton."

The church is warmed by Porritt's underground
hot-air apparatus, which was placed in the nave in
1885, at a cost of nearly £50.

Among other gifts to the restored church should
be mentioned a handsome frontal of green silk for
the holy table, embroidered and presented by Mrs.
Saunders, late of South Walsham Vicarage; and
some oak panelling inside the pulpit, in which is
skilfully introduced ancient oak tracery, saved from
the old seating of the church. This panelling is
the gift of Mr. W. Evans, South Walsham.

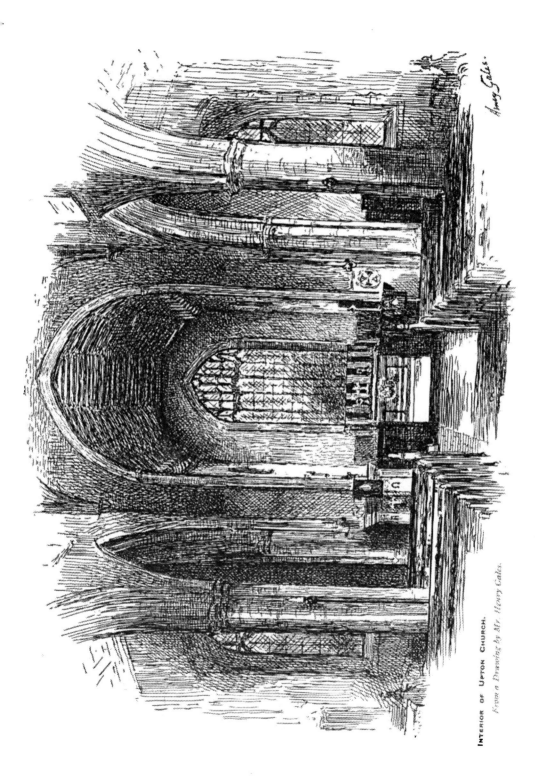

Amy Giles.

INTERIOR OF UPTON CHURCH.

From a Drawing by Mr. Henry Giles.

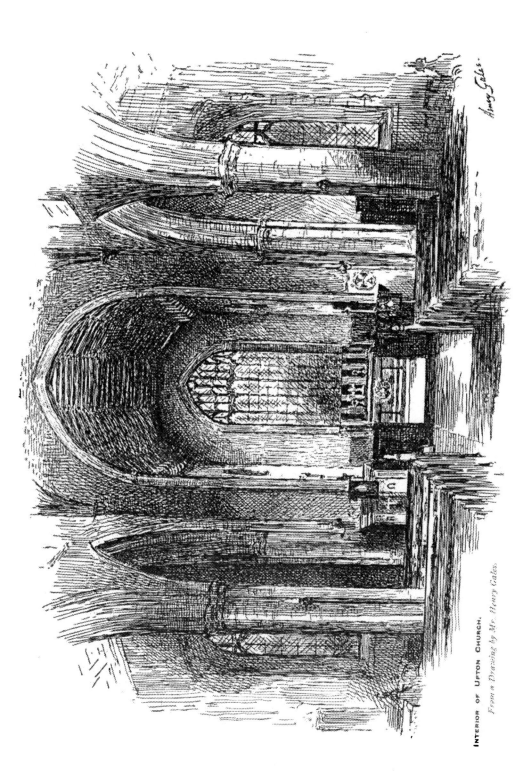

INTERIOR OF UPTON CHURCH.

From a Drawing by Mr. Henry Gates.

CHAPTER IV.

Of the Registers : curious Entries.

T HE Register dates from 1558, but the Date of Register, anno primo Elizabethæ. earliest part, as so often is the case, is a transcript, very well engrossed. I believe the original entries begin in 1606. There are some omissions from the first volume, the greatest hiatus occurring from 1685 to 1694. The period of the Commonwealth is marked by a change of handwriting, from the vicar's to that of a lay registrar, albeit the good vicar was allowed to record the baptism of his daughter with his own hand, which he does as follows :—

"Elizabeth, the daughter of Berney Sheppard
& Bridget his wife, was baptized the 6ᵗ
day of Nouēber, 1655."

Whether the troublous times proved too much for the vicar or not, certain it is that about fifteen months after the baptism of their infant daughter, both he and his wife Bridget died within a few days of each other, and were buried at Fishley. Mrs. Sheppard belonged to the Moundford family.

The following entries, including a civil marriage of the period, and its ecclesiastical completion (even at the time of the Commonwealth) by a clergyman, will be read with interest :—

" 1655.

Common-wealth Regis-ter. "The Register Booke of Upton containinge all Marriages, Byrthes, and Burialls accordinge to an Acte of pliam^t in that case cõmanded bearinge date the 24th of August, 1654.

"Robert Goat the elder was chosen pish Register by the Inħitants of the said towne, and sworne to the pformance of the said Office, and this day confirmed Register under my hande 1654.

"Gabr. Barbor.

Civil Marriage. "Robert Goat of Upton and Elizabeth Downes of Acle were married before me Gabriell Barbor, D^r in phisick, one of the Justices of the publique peace for the Countie of Norff., upon the ffift day of August one thousand sixe hundered ffifty &

ffower. In the p̃sence of John Downes, Edward Goate, and Charles Coppinge. Wittness my hande

> "Gabr. Barbor.

"The abovesaid Robert Goat of Vpton and Elizabeth Downes of Acle were marryed by me Philip Whitefoote, clerk, vpon yᵉ fift day of August, 1654, in the pʳsence of John Downes and Edward Goate. Witnesse my hande

> "Philip Whitefoote."

The Act of Charles II., intended to encourage the wool trade, is illustrated by the following extracts among others :— **Aot to foster the wool trade.**

| Burials in Upton since the 1st of August, 1678. Robert Smith, yᵉ sonne of Robert Smith, was buried yᵉ 29ᵗʰ of September. | Francis Hempson made oath before Robert Houghton, Justice of yᵉ Peace, yᵗ yᵉ coffin of yᵉ p contra Robert Smith was not faced with anything, and yᵗ his body was wrapt in a shroud of sheep's wool onelie. Dated yᵉ 4ᵗʰ day of October, 1678. Sealed and subscribed by those yᵗ were present at yᵉ swearing yᵉ affidavit. Simon Woodrowe and Robert Smith. |

John Mason, the sonne of Henrie Mason, was buried ye 8th of December.

Bridget Green made oath before Justice Haughton that when John Mason was buried theire was nothing in the coffin but what was made of sheep's wool, and the witnesses of ye affidavit were Thomas Noble and Henery Mason. Dated the 13th day of December.

1678. Robert Goodwinn, Clerke, was buried according to the Act the 12th day of februarie. Ebenezer Carter mad oath before Robt. Houghton, Esq.

Burials 1679. John, the son of Isaac Emperor of Norw^{ch}, was buried the 1st of September.

Bridget Manser made oath before Franc. Bacon, Esqr and Justice of Peace, that the said John Emperor was buried according to the full intent of the Act. Dated the 3^d of Sept., Anno Caroli Reg. 31º.

Excommunications. Records of excommunication occur in the register as late as the latter half of the seventeenth century.

"Memorandum that John Emperor of the Parish and Mannor of Upton St. Margarett was excommunicated by Robert Goodwyn, Clerk, and absolved by me, the sixth day of July, his successor and now p^rsent Vicar thereof, and this absolution pronounced in the yeare of o^r Lord, 1679,

"Saṁ Style."

John Emperor lived about a year and a half to enjoy his freedom from ecclesiastical censure, *vide* his will, page 121.

"Memord. that John Littlewood of Upton was excoṁunicated de non comparendo in Curiâ Ecclesiasticâ, March 25th, 168%, by me,

"Sam. Style, vic ibid."

A tax on the entries of births, burials, and marriages, temp. Geo. III., is noted, as follows:— **Duty payable on entries in Parish Register.**

"Dec. 9th, 1784.

"Duty ^rceived on the entry of all Births, Burials, and Marriages made in this Register Book for the parish of Upton from the first day of October, 1783, to the first day of Oct^r, 1784, amounting in the whole to the sum of five shillings and three pence.

"Received by me, Wm Brisley (?), for J. Gay, Juner, Collectere."

"Marryages in 1727.

"James Bensly and Suanna Barit were marryed the 11th May, 1727, the match by the parishtion^ors consentin to pay the charges of the marryage." **Marriage fees paid by the parish.**

Sibaret.
[Banns.]

"Benjamin Mundford and Anne Burre were Married May y⁰ 4ᵗʰ, 1721, wᵗʰ Sibaret."

A poetical
vicar.

The Rev. Wm. Mackay has left in the Register evidence of his love for Latin aphorisms, to wit:—

"Transivere Patres, simul hinc Transivimus Omnes.
In Cœlo Patriam, Qui Bene Transit, Habet.

Wm. Mackay, A.M.,

Parochiæ hujus Uptonensis Vicarius,
Apud Martham 24ᵗᵒ Junii,
Anno Xti 1729."

"Nulla Dies periat ; periat pars Nulla Dẽi
Nam tu sic peries, ut periere Dies.

Let no Day Pass, Pass no part of the Day,
For you must Pass, as Days do pass Away.
June 10ᵗʰ, 1736."

He has also recorded an epitaph for the benefit of posterity:—

"Our Life's the Shadow, God's the Pole,
the Index pointing, is Our Soul ;
Death's the Horison, where our sun must set,
Which will thro Xt A Resurrection get.

"W. M., Ap. 10th, 1732."

CHAPER V.

Of Monumental Inscriptions: Church and Churchyard.

S EVERAL brass inscriptions have been removed from the church in the past, empty matrices marking their former positions. The brasses remaining are as follow:—

PRE-REFORMATION BRASSES.

1. Orate p' aīa Thom'e Cossey de Upto' q' obiit riij° die mensis decembris A° Dni. m°cccc°lb° cui aīe p'piciet de'.
2. Orate p' aīab; Rob'ti Wynne et Agnetis ur. ei'.
3. Orate p' aīab; Rob'ti Dokkyg & Helwisie consortis sue.
4. Orate p' aīab; Willi. Wynne et Agnetis ur'is sue qui quidm Wills. obiit rrbiii die Octobris a° dni. m°b°b° quos aīab; ppciet de'.

5. 𝕺rate p' aïa Thom'ᵉ Wesyt, genosi, qui obiit xviii°
     die Augusti A° Dni. M°v°xiii cui aïe p'piciet de'.

6. 𝕺rate p' aïa Ihone taylour cui aïe p'piciet de'.

7. 𝕺rate p' aïa Roger' Tayler cui aïe p'piciet' de' a°
     r¹ xv°xxxiiij.

POST-REFORMATION BRASS.

Here lieth the bodie of Richard Taylor, who died the
xxix^th daye of September, A° 1588.

STONE INSCRIPTIONS.

[*Chancel. Mural tablet.*]

TO THE MEMORY OF
JOHN WATERS,
LATE OF UPTON HALL, FOR MANY YEARS A RESPECTED
INHABITANT, AND LORD OF THE MANOR OF UPTON.
DIED 16th APRIL, 1876,
AGED 87 YEARS.

[*Floor.*]   Sacred to the Memory of
WILLIAM WATERS,
Who departed this life September 25th, 1852,
Aged 90 years.

Sacred to the memory of
SAMUEL the Son of
WILLIAM and DINAH WATERS
Who departed this life August 22nd, 1846,
Aged 60 years.

Sacred to the Memory of
DINAH WATERS
the wife of WILLIAM WATERS
who departed this life September 4th, 1814,
Aged 53 years.

[*North chapel.   Mural tablets.*]

Sacred to the Memory of
JOHN HOLMES,
Many years an Inhabitant of this Parish,
Who departed this life Jan.ʸ 22ⁿᵈ, 1820, aged 69 years.
An honest Man's the noblest work of God.
Also ELIZABETH,
Second wife of the above, Died April 11ᵗʰ, 1848,
Aged 86 Yrˢ.

In Memory of
ELIZABETH HOLMES, the wife of
JOHN HOLMES of Upton,
and Daughter of
WILLᵐ & ELIZABETH COBB,
late of Hemblington in Norfolk,
who departed this Life June 26, 1796,
Aged 72 Years.

[*Floor.*]   Memento Mori.
In hope of a joyfull Resurrection,
Here Lyeth yᵉ Body of
Elz., Wife of
WILLIAM COBB, who dyed yᵉ 8ᵗʰ, 1726,
Aged 32 Years.

[*South chapel.   Floor.*]
Here lyeth
the body of
Edward Goate,
who dyed yᵉ
26 of Decm.,
1693.

[*South aisle.*]

Here lieth the Body of ROBERT GOAT, late
of this Parish ; who died December 2ᵈ, 1764,
Aged 81 Years.

In Memory of ROBERT GOAT, the Husband
of Elizabeth Goat, who departed this Life
Decembeʳ the 9ᵗʰ, 1772, Aged 64 Years.

In Memory of EDWᴰ GOAT, who departed
this Life February 11ᵗʰ, 1787, Aged 76 years.

In Memory of MARY, the Wife of
Thomas Baker,
and Daughter of Willᵐ & Mary Jay,
died Augⁿ yᵉ 16ᵗʰ, 1770, Aged 21 years.
Escap'd from every human ill, I fly
To meet my dear Redeemer in yᵉ sky ;
Happy exchange for sickness, grief, and pain,
A Crown of Bliss & endless joys to gain.

In Memory of William yᵉ son of James Jay,
Late of this Parish. He departed this life
February yᵉ 14ᵗʰ, 1765,
Aged 41 Years.

In memory of
James Jay,
who departed this life Janʳʸ yᵉ 17ᵗʰ, 1759, Aged 67 Years.
And Thomas, his Grand-Child, who died in his Infancy.
Also James, his Grand-Son, Who died March yᵉ 30ᵗʰ,
Aged 4 Years.
the Sons of Willᵐ & Mary Jay.

Here resteth ye Body of Mary, Daugh^{tr} of
James Jay, who died
April the 15th, 1741, Aged 21 Years.

In Memory of James, ye Son of James Jay,
Who died ye 25th Sept^r, 1752, Aged 29 Years.

[*Nave.*]   In Memory of
Thomas Jay
of Upton, in the County of Norfolk, who died 3rd of
November, 1797, Aged 80 Years.

SACRED
to the Memory of
MATILDA
Daughter of
THO^s & MARY ANNE
CLARKE,
Who died Sep^{tr} 1st, 1832, in the 8th Year of Her Age.
ALSO
three of their Sons, who died in their Infancy.

To the Memory of
Martha, ye Wife of Robert Whaites,
Who departed this Life April the 18th, 1743,
Aged 28 years.   Also James, their Son, Died an Infant.

In Memory of
George Docking,
Who Departed this Life May 10th, 1779, Aged 77 Years.

Here [lieth the] Body of Jacob Docking, Son of George
Docking & Ann his Wife, who died Sep. 27th, 1736,
Aged 16.

In Memory of Ann, the wife of George Docking,
who departed this Life 3rd of Feb^y, 1778. Aged 80 Years.

[*North aisle.*]

Sacred to the Memory of
Isaac Docking,
Late of Upton, Who died Novr 28th, 1807,
In the 75 Year of his Age.
Also
Mary his wife, who died March 29th, 1836, Aged 72 Years.

Sacred to the Memory of George, Son of George
& Mary Docking of this Parish, who died
July 19th, 1827, Aged 40 Years,
And Great-Grandson of the late George Docking.

Sacred
to the Memory of MARY DOCKING, the Wife of
GEORGE DOCKING, who departed this life
7th October, 1841,
Aged 78 Years.

Sacred to the Memory of
GEORGE DOCKING,
Many years a proprietor, and an inhabitant of
this Parish. Who departed this life
Feb. 23rd 1837,
Aged 78 Years.
An honest man's the noblest work of God.

Notes of all the Legible Monumental Inscriptions in the Churchyard of Upton.

South Side of Church.   South of Main Pathway.

James Grimble, late of Blofield, d. Feb. 13th, 1838, 70 yrs.

Samuel, son of James and Elizabeth Betts, d. Sep. 12th, 1866, 20 yrs.

James Betts, husb. of Judith Betts, d. 28th Aug., 1844, 77 yrs. Also Judith, wife, 18th Sep., 1860, 78 yrs.

Benjamin, son of James and Martha Willgress, d. Aug. 18th, 1836, 16 yrs.

Samuel Bunn, ob. May 15th, 1838, Æ. 60. Also Sarah Crawford, daugh. of the above, ob. March 12th, 1835, Æ. 26.

Charlotte Page d. 14th June, 1835, 20 yrs.

William Page d. 31st May, 1820, 40 yrs. Also Sarah his wife, d. 19th Aug., 1818, 37 yrs. And of Sarah Tower Page, their daugh., d. Oct. 27th, 1829, 18 yrs.

Elizth., wife of James Porter of this parish, d. 10th May, 1823, 67 yrs.

James Porter d. 6th Apr., 1842, 94 yrs.

William, son of Charles and Sarah George, and grandson of Joseph and Rachel Browne, d. 11th Aug., 1828, 21 yrs.

Rachel Browne d. Sep. 8th, 1846, 91 yrs.

Jacob Day d. Mar. 15th, 1820, 67 yrs.

Thomas Day d. Feb. 7th, 1781, 87 yrs. Also Martha, wife, d. June 24th, 1787, 73 yrs.

Mary, dau. of Joseph and Rachel Browne, d. July 10th, 1802, in 12th yr.

G

Joseph Browne, husb. of Rachel Browne, d. Oct. 26th, 1817, 73 yrs.

John Howard d. 13th Mar., 1842, 81 yrs. Also Amy Howard, wife, 1st Sept., 1837, 74 yrs. Also Amy Howard, daugh., d. 2nd Feb., 1810, 18 yrs.

Robert Willgress d. 14th Feb., 1813, 78 yrs. Also Amy, wife, d. 16th June, 1804, 63 years. And Benj., son, d. 1st June, 1799, 25 years.

Benj. Tungate d. Jan. 11th, 1814, 69 years. Also Susannah, wife, Jan. 22nd, 1814, 64 years.

Benjn. Tongate, son of Benj. and Susanna Tongate, d. June 4th, 1804, 28 yrs.

William, husb. of Green Farman, d. Feb. 5th, 1821, 55 yrs.

Joseph, son of William and Green Farman, d. 4th May, 1830, 26 yrs.

> Remember me as you pass by.
> As you are now, so once was I ;
> As I am now, so must you be :
> Therefore, prepare to follow me.

William Turner d. Oct. 10th, 1796, 68 yrs. Also Mary, wife, d. Mar. 14th, 1804, 73 yrs.

John Turner d. Aug. 12th, 1832, 59 yrs. Also Mary, wife, d. May 20th, 1859, 86 yrs.

John Davy d. Aug. 2nd, 1833, 31 yrs. Sarah, his wife, d. May 11th, 1837, 32 yrs.

John, son of John and Sarah Davey, d. at Melville Naval Hospital, Feb. 7th, 1857, 28 yrs. Also William, their son, d. on his passage from China, Nov. 16th, 1857, 24 yrs.

> May we all meet at the resurrection of the just.

Mary, wife of Joseph Howes, d. Dec. 4th, 1860, age 68.

Isaac Bradford d. July 31st, 1841, 46 yrs. Martha, wife, d. 27th Nov., 1841, 47 yrs.

Robert, son of John and Mary Turner, d. July 14th, 1835, 26 yrs. Also Edward, their son, died in infancy.

Jane Mary, dau. of George and Jane Turner, d. July 5th, 1846, 13 months.

Jane, wife of George Maddle Turner, d. June 24th, 1873, 68 yrs. Also George Maddle Turner, husb. of above, d. May 4th, 1883, 76 yrs.

Emma Sales, dau. of Mary Ann Gilling, d. 21st Oct., 1840, 20 yrs.

W. George d. Mar. 23rd, 1860, 1 year.

Robert Beverley, husb. of Mary Beverley, d. Nov. 25th, 1853, 67 yrs.

Mary, wife of Robert Beverley, d. July 15th, 1832, 50 yrs.

Willm. Florence d. 20th Oct., 1789, 73 yrs.

Mary, wife of Willm. Florrance of Upton, d. 25th Jan., 1784, 66 yrs. Also William, their son, d. 15th May, 1760, 13 yrs.

Charlotte Davey, wife of John Davey, d. 2nd Apr., 1838, 64 yrs. Also John Davey, husb., d. 23rd June, 1840, 71 yrs.

John Ewlls Davey, husb. of Sarah Ann Davey, d. 30th Dec., 1843, 35 yrs.

John Ellis d. 1st Jan., 1796, 42 yrs. Also Elizth., wife, d. 14th Feb., 1813, 55 yrs.

Noah Norton d. Dec. 21st, 1759, 46 yrs.

William, son of Edmund and Elizth. Harrison, d. 19th June, 1826, 30 yrs. Also John, their son, d. 13th Mar., 1829, 40 yrs.

Edmund Harrison d. 26th Jan., 1840, 79 yrs. Also Elizabeth, wife, d. 22nd Oct., 1841, 78 yrs.

Arabella Maria Sutton, widow, d. 11th Nov., 1869, 74 yrs.

Benjn., husb. of Francis Skyles, d. Jan. 26th, 1824, 25 yrs.

Children of Adam and Sarah Waters. George, d. Sep. 28th, 1844, 5 yrs. Sarah, d. Feb. 25th, 1845, 10 yrs.

Isabella, wife of Joseph Stout, d. vth June, MDCCCXXVI,
aged XXXVI yrs. Also eight of their children, who
died infants. Also Joseph Stout, husband of above,
d. 24th Mar., 1837, 52 yrs.

Thomas Stout d. Dec. 17th, 1861, 72 yrs. Also Theodosia
Harbord d. May 8th, 1883, 81 yrs.

Simon Stout of this Parish, d. Feb. 11th, 1823, 77 yrs.
Also Isabella, wife, d. Mar. 27th, 1825, 84 yrs.

Thomas Stoutt d. 14th Oct., 1838, 86 years. Also Jane
Stoutt, wife, d. 30th Aug., 1841. Also Priscilla Stoutt,
d. 17th May, 1847, 47 yrs.

Susanna Homes d. 14th Aug., 1848, 56 yrs.

John Neale d. Feb. 16th, 1768, 58 yrs.

Susan, wife of John Neale, d. 3rd Apr., 1779, 70 yrs.

Nicholas, husb. of Rose Kerrison, d. 27th Mar., 1822, 46 yrs.

John Mendham, husb. of Elizabeth Mendham, d. Nov. 25th,
1718, 36 yrs. 2 months.

David Taylor, husb. of Frances Taylor, d. July 5th, 1856,
65 yrs. Also Frances Taylor, wife of above, d. Feb.
2nd, 1859, 71 yrs.

Fredc. Huke Taylor, d. Feb. 26th, 1858, 9 months. Also
Albert Abraham Taylor, d. Feb. 18th, 1861, 5 months.

Elizabeth, wife of Robert Dingle, d. July 10th, 1775, 47 yrs.
Also Robert Dingle, d. May 29th, 1789, 69 yrs.

Robert Read, husb. of Sarah Ann Read, d. May 10th, 1882,
76 yrs.

Thomas Diamond d. 17th Ap., 1801, 66 yrs.

Hannah, daug. of Thomas and Margaret Creak, d. July
22nd, 1740, 22 yrs.

Robert, husb. of Mary Smith, d. Jan. 11th, 1821, 87 yrs.
Also John, son of above and husb. of Elizth. Smith, d.
June 11th, 1825, 46 yrs.

Sarah, wife of Robert Agus, and daug. of Robert and Mary

Smith, d. 24th Sep., 1849, 58 yrs. Also Robert Agus, d. Sep. 19th, 1868, 75 yrs. Also Mary Ann Mingay, their daugh., died at Edinburgh, Scotland, Aug. 30th, 1868, 40 yrs.

North of Main Pathway.

John Cater, husb. of Margaret Cater, d. Aug. 19th, 1861, 69 yrs.

> A Better Husband never liv'd,
> A Kinder Father never died;
> His honest heart no man deceived,
> His manly spirit knew no pride.
> His memory fondly in our hearts shall rest,
> Lov'd while on earth, in heaven for ever blest.

Also of Margaret, wife, "who fell asleep in Jesus," June 6th, 1876, 82 yrs.

Willm. Cater d. Sep. 20th, 1855, 75 yrs.

George Westgate, son of Robert and Elizth. Westgate, d. Feb. 4th, 1832, 37 yrs.

William Cater, d. Feb. 9th, 1842, in 87th year.

> "Life is uncertain, Death is sure;
> Sin is the cause, Christ can cure."

Ann, wife of Willm. Cater, d. Ap. 23rd, 1846, in 87th yr.

John Tungate d. 13th Oct., 1821, 84 yrs. Also Ann, wife, d. 20th May, 1826, 80 yrs.

Robert Tungate, husb. of Elizth. Tungate, d. Aug. 8th, 1807, 84 yrs. Benj. Tungate, husb. of Sarah Tungate, d. Aug. 27th, 1808, 87 yrs.

Mary Diamand, daugh. of Robert and Elizth. Westgate, d. Oct. 8th, 1822, 35 yrs.

Elizth. Westgate, wife of Robert Westgate of this parish d. July 11th, 1829, 82 yrs.

Jacob, son of Robert and Sarah Hilling, d. Ap. 13th, 1784, 37 yrs.

Edward, son of Edward and Ann Goffin, d. Sep. 23rd, 1784, 40 yrs.

Robt. Hilling d. Oct. yᵉ 25th, 1770, 78 yrs.   Also Sarah, wife, d. July yᵉ 18th, 1771, 64 yrs.

Charles Robert Baldock, Lieut. Royal Artillery, d. 26th Jan., 1858, 65 yrs.

John Hilling, son of Robt. and Sarah Hilling, d. June 11th, 1769, aged 39.

[*Mitchell tomb.*]   John Littlewood of this parish, farmer, d. 20th Apr., 1756, 59 yrs. Ann, wife, d. 10th Nov., 1783, 84 yrs. Samuel Mitchell obt. Oct. 14th, 1859, 86 yrs. Averill Sibell obt. Sep. 28th, 1860, 80 yrs. William Mitchell obt. Feb. 13th, 1865, 53 yrs.

[*Sibel and Cater tomb.*]   William Sibel d. 26th Feb., 1830, 41 yrs. Charlotte, wife of William Sibel, only daugh. of Edmund and Elizth. Cater, d. 24th Feb., 1828, 36 yrs., and infant daughter. Edmund Cater of South Walsham d. Mar. 17th, 1832, 75 yrs. Elizabeth, wife of Edmund Cater, daugh. of John and Amy Mitchell of this parish, d. 28th Apr., 1826, 64 yrs.

Adam Wright, husb. of Mary Wright, d. Sep. 9th, 1792, 76 yrs.

> " I've tasted of pleasure, I've tasted of pain,
> And found by experience this life is but vain,
> So now I take leave of its sorrow and joy,
> For God hath appointed that all men must die.

> " And seeing 'tis meant with a gracious design,
> My natural body to dust I resign—
> I hope when my soul shall ascend to the skies,
> I shall in a spiritual body arise."

Elizabeth, daugh. of Thos. and Elizth. Dawson, d. in infancy,
8th Apr., 1788.

Enoch England, husb. of Elizth. England, d. July 23rd,
1786, 49 yrs.

Thos. Day, late of this parish, d. Mar. 31st, 1836, 84 yrs.
Also Elizth., wife, d. Jan. 10th, 1829, 77 yrs.

Thomas Day d. Mar. 25th, 1794, 80 yrs.
"The frowns of the world are with him at an end,
Exchanged for the smiles of his Saviour and Friend.
Escaped from the regions of sorrow and woe,
Affliction and trouble no more he shall know."

Isaac, son of Thos. and Elizth. Day, d. 24th Aug., 1782, 12
yrs.

Diana, daugh. of Willm. and Diana Waters, d. June 27th,
1799, 1 year.

[In East Wall of South Aisle.]

John Cater d. 12th Oct., 1781, 59 years.
"Afflictions sore long time I bore,
Physicians were in vain,
Till God was pleased to give me ease,
And free me from my pain."

Also Ann Cater, wife, d. June 18th, 1804, 72 years.

Two graves near have footstones marked "A.C." and "J.C."

Enoch Cater d. 14th Jan., 1868, 70 yrs.

Mrs. Elizth. Meadows d. 16th May, 1833, 57 yrs. "She
was an affectionate Wife, a tender Mother, and a sincere
Friend."

[*Capon tomb.*] Rebecca Susannah, d. of Robert and
Rebecca Capon, d. 17th Jan., 1858, 13 yrs. Mary Ann,
infant daugh., d. 1851. Robert Capon, d. Dec. 4th,
1882, 68 yrs. Rebecca, wife, March 25th, 1886, 69 yrs.
Elizabeth Susannah Cowles (sister of last named) d.

Apr. 15th, 1887, 62 yrs.   Susannah Postle d. 16th Jan., 1862, 75 yrs. Also Susannah, only daugh. of above, d. June 13th, 1864, 43 yrs.

Elizabeth, wife of John Barker, d. Oct. 28th, 1765, 81 yrs.

Mary Day, d. 11th June, 1849, 71 yrs.

Ellen, wife of Thomas Day, d. 20th Mar., 1774, 49 yrs. Also Matthew, their son, d. 16th June, 1771, 16 yrs.

Sarah, wife of John Clare, d. 28th May, 1800, 60 yrs.

" Reader, remember thou must die,
And turn to dust as well as I ;
Repent thy own misconduct past,
And thou't be happy at the last."

Ann, wife of William Maddle, d. Jan. 29th, 1793, 55 yrs.

John Day, late of this Parish, d. Oct. 28th, 1840, 49 yrs. Also Jane, wife, d. Nov. 9th, 1841, 44 yrs.

Elizth., wife of Charles Francis, d. Apr. 6th, 1821, 47 yrs.

Charles Francis, husb. of Elizth., d. July 8th, 1814, 54 yrs.

Benj. Francis d. Aug. 24th, 1814, in 70th yr.

Frances, wife of Benj. Francis, d. Sep. 21st, 1798, 77 yrs.

Benj. Francis, husb. of Frances, d. May 2nd, 1792, 81 yrs.

Elizabeth, dau. of Benj. and Frances Francis, d. Dec. 25th, 1770, 20 yrs.

Charles Francis d. 24th July, 1758, 77 yrs.

[*Dawson tomb.*]   Thomas Dawson d. 2nd Dec., 1803, 76 yrs. Ann Dawson, wife, d. 14th Dec., 1810, 89 yrs.

[*Brown tomb.*] James Brown d. 8th Aug., 1828, 72nd yr. Elizth., his wife, d. 24th Jan., 1837, 70th yr. Susan Skoyles, their daugh., wife of Samuel Skoyles, d. 1st July, 1828, 30th yr.

Wm. Henry, son of Jas. and Susanna Brown, d. Nov. 17th, 1872, 37 yrs.

Henry Dawson Brown d. Jan. 13th, 1875, 68 yrs. Elizth.

English, wife of Hen. Dawson Brown, eldest daugh. of late Robt. Beverley, d. Nov. 14th, 1881, 68 yrs.

Enoch Brown d. Nov. 25th, 1831, 35 yrs. James Brown d. Oct. 31st, 1856, 61 yrs.

Edgar Samuel Munford d. Sep. 23rd, 1867, 4 yrs.

Elizth., wife of Benj. Munford, d. June 19th, 1853, 82nd yr.

Benj. Munford, husb. of Eliz. Munford, d. Mar. 2nd, 1861, 93rd yr.

John, husb. of Eliz. Dawson Turner, d. Nov. 24th, 1868, 70 yrs.

Rebecca, wife of Joseph Munford, d. Oct. 5th, 1799, 70 yrs. Also two grandchildren, infants.

Joseph Munford d. June 26th, 1789, 56 yrs.

John Curson d. 7th Oct., 1811, 70 yrs.

Danl. Curson d. 13th Jan., 1773, 73 yrs. Mary his wife, d. 19th Apr., 1772, 75 yrs.

Daughters of Jas. and Charlotte Porter: Mary, d. Apr. 22nd, 1867, 12 yrs. Charlotte Elizabeth, d. May 14th, 1867, 15 yrs. Maria, d. May 15th, 1867, 18 yrs. (Three stones.)

Mary, dau. of Mark and Maria Porter, wife of Simeon Smith, d. July 6th, 1864, 35 yrs.

William, son of Mary Porter, d. June 25th, 1864, 18 yrs.

Mark Porter, husb. of Maria Porter, d. 16th Feb., 1852, 55 yrs.

Maria, wife of Mark Porter, d. Dec. 8th, 1885, 85 yrs.

[*Waters tomb.*] William Waters d. Nov. 1st, 1859, 68 yrs., 4th son of William and Dinah Waters. Mark Waters, eldest son of William and Dinah Waters of this parish, d. Dec. 18th, 1862, 75 yrs. Sarah Waters, dau. of Wm. and Dinah, d. May 7th, 1871, 78 yrs. Benj. Waters, 6th son of Wm. and Dinah, d. Feb. 4th, 1867, 66 yrs. John Waters, 3rd son of Wm. and Dinah, d. Apr. 16th,

1876, 87 yrs. William Waters, only son of Azariah and Mary Anne Waters of Hoe Lodge, East Dereham, d. at Halvergate House, June 10th, 1880, 34 yrs.

Jasper Gaze d. 17th Nov., 1882, 57 yrs. Jasper Mitchell Gaze d. 13th Sept. 1869, 4 yrs. and 10 mths.

William Gaze d. June 7th, 1875, 78 yrs. Margaret, wife of Wm. Gaze, d. Nov. 10th, 1864, 72 yrs.

Ann Fabb, infant dau. of Samuel and Mary Bracey, b. Mar. 13th, 1840 ; d. Aug. 10th, 1840.

George Grimmer, son of William and Maria Grimmer of Fishley Hall, d. Feb. —, 1842, 10 mths.

John Nickels d. Jan. 19th, 1825, 77 yrs.

Frances, wife of Wm. Hood, d. 31st July, 1827, 85 yrs.

William Hood, husb. of Frances Hood, d. Oct. 16th, 1817, 75 yrs.

Sarah, wife of Thos. Wiseman, d. 9th Nov., 1866, 78 yrs. Thos. Wiseman d. 22nd Jan., 1872, 82 yrs.

[Broken stone.] . . . gate . . . Oct. 13th, 1821 . . . . (Register.—1821. John Tungate, buried Oct. 17th, 85 yrs.)

Susannah, wife of James Hood, d. Sept. 13th, 1865, 80th yr.

James Hood d. Sep. 27th, 1874, 89th yr. William Hood, his son, who d. in the harvest field, Aug. 11th, 1873, 50 yrs.

Wm. Gillings, husb. of Hannah Gillings, d. June 7th, 1861, 51 yrs.

Robert Cockerill d. Feb. 26th, 1824, 86 yrs. Also Elizabeth his wife, d. Feb. 6th, 1822, 64 yrs.

John Helsdon, husb. of Maria Helsdon, b. Oct. 10th, 1818; d. May 26th, 1868.

Maria Helsdon, wife of above, d. Aug. 27th, 1885, 60 yrs.

James Christmas, son of William and Sarah Odell, b. Dec. 25th, 1837 ; d. June 16th, 1863.

Priscilla Allen d. of William and Theodosia Harbord, d. June 6th, 1853, 24 yrs.

Henry, son of Wm. and Theodosia Harbord, d. Nov. 19th, 1855, 17 yrs.

Alice, wife of Thos. Kirk, d. Jan. 29th, 1870, 68 yrs.

Thomas Chamberlin d. May 17th, 1858, 73 yrs.   Mary Chamberlin, his wife, d. Oct. 11th, 1870, 80 yrs. Robert Chamberlin d. Oct. 17th, 1855, 5 yrs.

Mary Ann Chamberlin, eldest dau. of James and Mary Ann Chamberlin, d. at Great Yarmouth, Jan. 3rd, 1873, 18 yrs.

James Chamberlin, husb. of Mary Ann Chamberlin, d. Mar. 19th, 1878, 62 yrs.

Elizabeth Chamberlin, wife of Thomas Chamberlin, d. Mar. 21st, 1886, 33 yrs.

Mary Ann, wife of James Chamberlin, d. May 24th, 1888, 67 yrs.

West of Church.

Thos. Dawson, husb. of Hannah Dawson, d. Oct. 8th, 1874, 76 yrs.

Catherine, wife of Thos. Dawson, d. May 10th, 1873, 81 yrs.

James Wiseman, b. at Upton, Aug. 24th, 1794; d. Apr. 16th, 1878.

Stephen Bately Ecclestone d. Oct. 5th, 1845, 49 yrs.

William Davey, husb. of Harriet Davey, d. Feb. 24th, 1887, 73 yrs.

Harriet Davey, wife of William Davey, b. Jan. 1st, 1819, d. Jan. 13th, 1889.

Sarah Ninham d. Sep. 29th, 1848, 62 yrs.

Harriet Davey d. 29th June, 1859, 20 yrs.   James Davey d. 20th Feb., 1851, 4 yrs. 8 mths.

James Willgress d. Aug. 3rd, 1887, 72 yrs.

John Daniels Willgress of this parish, d. 13th July, 1880, 72 yrs.

[*Willgress tomb.*]   Martha Willgress d. Nov. 25th, 1869, 84 yrs. James Willgress d. Jan. 4th, 1871, 86 yrs. Jonathan Daniel Willgress, husb. of Julia Ann Willgress, d. Apr. 9th, 1879, 53rd yr.

Edward, son of William and Sarah Rogers, d. Jan. 17th, 1718, 4 yrs. 3 mths.

Benjamin Walter, son of Benj. and Ann Watts, d. Mar. 16th, 1887, 3 yrs.

Geo. Riches d. Apr. 22nd, 1860, 62 yrs.

C. Smith d. July 26th, 1863, 6 mths.

Violet Georgiana, dau. of Wm. and Sarah Mitchell, d. Sep. 26th, 1877, 1 yr.   William, infant son, d. July 18th, 1866, 3 wks.

John Smith, husb. of Sarah Smith, d. Sep. 22nd, 1877, 59 yrs.   Their children: Charles, d. July 26th, 1863, 4 yrs. Eliza, d. Nov. 6th, 1863, 22 yrs.   Henry, d. Feb. 21st, 1866, 19 yrs.

Ann Maria, dau. of James and Ann Dawson, d. Oct. 30th, 1867, 15 yrs.

Emily, wife of Robert Allen, d. Apr. 17th, 1866, 44 yrs.

Ann Harriet, dau. of Robert and Emily Allen, d. Nov. 10th, 1872, 20 yrs.

John Allen, husb. of Ann Allen, d. Apr. 9th, 1881, 90th yr.

Margaret Gibbs Hood, eldest dau. of late Jas. and Susan Anna Hood, d. Dec. 21st, 1887, 71 yrs.

John Smith, husb. of Caroline Smith, d. Dec. 15th, 1887, 30 yrs.

Charles Smith d. Nov. 15th, 1869, 8 mths.   Also Sarah Elizabeth, d. Nov. 17th, 1869, 3 yrs. 3 mths.   Children of Robert and Maria Smith.

Susannah T. Hall, dau. of Mary Ann Davies, d. Mar. 2nd, 1883, 43 yrs.

John Turner, son of Elizabeth Dawson Turner, d. Oct. 15th,
    1883, 54 yrs. Respected by all who knew him.
Elizabeth Munford, wife of Samuel Munford, dau. of
    Elizabeth Dawson Turner, d. May 7th, 1883, 52 yrs.
Elizabeth, wife of John Kendall of Runham, d. Jan. 15th,
    1876, 61 yrs.
Benj. Adams, husb. of Mary Ann Adams, d. July 26th, 1874,
    74 yrs. Also Mary Ann, his wife, d. Dec. 21st, 1882,
    75 yrs.
Hannah Gook, wife of Wm. Gook, d. June 4th, 1878, 39 yrs.
James Betts, husb. of Eliz. Betts of this parish, d. Feb. 15th,
    1882, 70th yr.
Robert Smith, husb. of Maria Smith, d. Jan. 30th, 1888,
    61 yrs.
Alfred G. Dove, d. Aug. 9th, 1886, 2 yrs. 6. mths.
Wm. Alexander, husb. of Elizabeth Alexander, d. June 7th,
    1886, 60 yrs.

Inscriptions on Stones about to be erected, 1891.

James Betts, husb. of Elizabeth Betts of this parish, d. Feb.
    15th, 1882, 70th yr. Also Elizabeth, wife, d. Nov. 14th,
    1888, 72 yrs.
George Turner, husb. of Elizabeth Turner, d. Feb. 18th,
    1889, 51 yrs.
James Benjamin Howes, husb. of Charlotte Anne Howes, d.
    Dec. 10th, 1889, 29 yrs.
Susannah Brown d. 31st May, 1889, 91 yrs.

CHAPTER VI.

Of the Parish : Churchwardens, National School, Vicarage House, and Miscellanea.

THE following list of churchwardens is obviously incomplete ; but, owing, alas! to the disappearance of the old church-wardens' books, I have been largely dependent on the Terriers (of which a good number exist at the Diocesan Registry), records in the Archdeacon's Registry, and the Parish Registers, for the names prior to 1850.

DATE.	CHURCHWARDENS.
1549.	William Doraunt and Simon Whetley.
1550.	Letters of sequestration of fruits of perpetual vicarage of the parish

church of Upton, now vacant, granted
to Robert Benslyn of Walsham St.
Lawrence, John Bullock, and John
Baker of Upton.—Consistorial Act
Book, Norwich, 1549—1555.

1551. John Wynne and Christopher Bullok.

1552-3. (?) John Ramsey and Edmund Tayllor.

1597. Robert Taylor and Robert ffisher.

1600-1. William Win and Christopher Gote.

1603. Robert Browne and Rich. Gymmingham.

1604-5. Robert Greene and John Bullocke.

1606. Gregory Goate and James Benslynge.

1607. Gregory Goate and Robert Greene.

1610. John Winne.

1614-15. John Benslynge and William Goate.

1627. James Taylor and Thomas Creake, sen.

1634. William Gote and John Gote.

1666. William Cooke and William Norton.

1678. Robert Greene and Robert Thompson.

1682. William Cobb and James Smyth.

1699. John Norton.

1706. James Skyner and John Norton, jun.

1709. Thomas Day and Charles Bullock.

1711. S. Jarmy.

1716. Samuel Jarmy and John Norton.

1721. Charles Bullock.

1723. Charles Bullock.

1725. Charles Bullock and John Norton.

1727.   Robert Goate and John Norton.
1728.   John Norton.
1729.   Robert Goate and Christopher Jay.
1733.   James Jay and Robert Hilling.
1735.   Robert Goate and James Jay.
1736.   James Jay and Robert Goate.
1740.   James Jay and Robert Hilling.
1747.   James Jay and Robert Whaites.
1760.   Thomas Jay and Robert Goat.
1763.   Robert Goat.
1770.   Robert Goat.
1777.   John Mitchell.
1784.   Thos. Jay and John Mitchell.
1791.   John Mitchell.
1794.   John Mitchell.
1801.   Charles Francis.
1806.   Charles Francis.
1813.   Charles Francis.
1820.   William Waters.
1827.   William Waters.
1834.   William Waters and John Waters.
1845.   John Waters.
1850-63. John Waters and William Mitchell.
1863-67. Robert Capon and Jasper Gaze.
1867-71. Robert Capon and James B. Parker.
1871-74. James B. Parker and Jasper Gaze.
1874-77. Jasper Gaze and Samuel Munford.
1877-8.   Jasper Gaze and John Broom.

1878-82. Jasper Gaze and William Partridge Cubitt.
  1883. William Partridge Cubitt.
1883-4. John Allen and Charles Bert Smith.
1884-8. John Allen and Michael Brown.
1888-9. Mary Ann Broom and Eliza Gaze.
1889-91. Eliza Gaze.

NATIONAL SCHOOL.

The philanthropic interest of Miss Edwards
of Hardingham Lodge, the chief landowner of
Fishley, was aroused on behalf of the children of
Upton more than twenty-one years ago. An
elementary school had, before that time, been
carried on under the management of the vicar
(the Rev. J. W. Greaves) and Mr. John Waters
(the chief landowner), in a school-room which
belonged to Mr. Waters. This school had, however, proved inadequate for the needs of the
parish ; and the managers very gladly welcomed
Miss Edwards' support, and placed the room at
her disposal. The first important step Miss
Edwards took was to send Miss Harwood—and,
six months later, Miss Gentleman, as her assis-
tant—to begin the good work which, for the
past twenty-one years, they have continuously
carried on, to the very great benefit of the parish.

H

Eventually, as the numbers of the children increased, Miss Edwards offered to build a new school, if the parish would provide a site and £150 towards the cost. This was readily done; and the present National School, with house attached, was erected in 1872, at an outlay by Miss Edwards of nearly £1000. The building was picturesquely designed by the Rev. J. Barham Johnson; and an excellent gymnasium was erected in the play-ground.

For many years Miss Edwards provided all necessary funds beyond the Government grant and school pence; and although, since 1880, the parish has contributed the small sum of £40 a year, she nobly bears the balance of the annual deficit.

The school is vested in the vicar and churchwardens of the parish for the time being, and is the property of the Church of England. The vicar is, *ex officio*, a manager, and chairman of the committee of management. The first two managers appointed by the deed to act with the vicar were Miss Edwards and Mr. John Squire. The elective managers, are required, before taking part in the management, to make the following declaration before the chairman :—" I, A. B., do hereby solemnly and sincerely declare that I am, and have been for three years last past, a member of the Church of England."

THE VICARAGE HOUSE.

An early record of an Archdeacon's Visitation gives the following reference to the then existing vicarage.

"1585, Upton. The Vicaredg howses are in great decay, for they are redye to fall downe, culpa vicarij."

The subjoined entry occurs in a terrier, preserved in the Diocesan Registry, made in the year 1845:—

"The following properties were sold in 1821 to redeem the land-tax, that is to say—

	A.	R.	P.
The vicarage house & scite (*sic*)	0	1	28
Turf land & water (No. 7) ...	1	2	0
„ „ (No. 8) ...	0	2	0
Containing in all ...	2	1	28 "

The above vicarage house is now a very small cottage situate near the Cock Inn, and is part of the property of the late John Waters, Esq.

The new vicarage house was built in the year 1887 (that of Queen Victoria's Jubilee), from the designs of Mr. A. S. Hewitt, architect. The Ecclesiastical Commissioners, who receive the great tithe, made a free grant of £1,500 towards the cost. This corporation also granted and conveyed, free of cost, the site containing 0a. 3r. 14p., which was the only piece of rectorial glebe they had in the parish. This piece of land adjoining the churchyard was formerly the site of the Tithe Barn, called in an old MS., which is preserved with the Parish Award, the " Tythe Barn Piece."

The recent discovery of ancient pottery in the vicarage garden, having the appearance of Anglo-Saxon funeral urns (in fragments), suggests the possibility of the site having been an Anglo-Saxon burial ground a thousand years ago.

MISCELLANEA.

NORFOLK POLL, 1714.

Upton, Walsham Hundred.

FREEHOLDERS.	RESIDENCE.	FREEHOLDERS.	RESIDENCE.
Bird, Joseph,	Norwich.	King, Charles,	Norwich.
Bullock, John.		Kipping, John,	Boyton.
Cobb, William,	Freethorp.	Nelson, Henry, clerk,	[Rockland.
Cooks, Henry,	Horstead.	Norton, John.	
Day, John.		Rogers, William.	
Jay, James.		Wing, William.	

The candidates for Parliament at this election were Sir Ralph Hare, Bart., Erasmus Earle, Esq.,

Sir Jacob Astley, Bart., and Thomas de Grey, Esq., and the Upton votes were equally distributed between them.

NORFOLK POLL, 1802. UPTON.

VOTER.	PLACE OF FREEHOLD.	OCCUPIER.
Allen, Robt.	... Upton ...	Himself.
Brown, James	... S.Walsham...	J. Codling.
Curson, John	... Upton ...	Himself.
Clair, John	... Acle... ...	S. Mallett.
Cator, Wm.	... Upton ...	Himself.
Clarke, John	.. Hindringham	G. Waters.
Davey, John	... Upton ...	Himself.
Diamond, Thos. ...	" ...	"
Dawson, Thos. ...	" ...	"
Day, Thos. ...	" ...	"
Day, Jacob ...	" ...	"
Docking, Isaac ...	" ...	"
Francis, William ...	" ...	C. Francis.
Holmes, John ...	" ...	Himself.
Maddle, Wm. ...	" ...	"
Riches, John ...	" ...	"
Smith, Robert ...	" ...	"
Stout, Simon ...	" ...	"
Tungate, John ...	" ...	"
Waters, Wm. ...	" ...	"
Whaites, John ...	" ...	"

Candidates for the election, Sir Jacob Henry Astley, Bart., Melton Constable; Thomas William Coke, Esq., Holkham; Hon. John Wodehouse, Witton Park. A joint address was issued by the two first-named, who were the retiring members. Mr. Coke had represented the county in four Parliaments, and had opposed Lord North's Administration and the American War. Since the coalition of 1783 he had been a supporter of Fox, and an open enemy of Pitt and his colleagues. The Hon. John Wodehouse, eldest son of Lord Wodehouse, came forward as a supporter of Mr. Pitt. Upton went strongly for Wodehouse, and Pitt's Administration, voting nineteen to two in his favour. Result of election, Astley, 3,612 votes; Coke, 4,317; Wodehouse, 3,517. An objection was made to the vote of John Clark of Upton, one of Wodehouse's supporters, on the ground that he was not assessed. The vote was held to be bad.

Population of Upton with Fishley, 1821, 66 houses, 241 males, 224 females, total population, 465. In 1881, the inhabitants of Upton alone numbered 508.

In a South Walsham rate made 4th March, 1677, for a copy of which I am indebted to J. E. T.

Pollard, Esq., South Walsham Rectory, the following
are rated as "outsetters":—"Upton. Roger Cope-
man, George Bird, Esq., Will. Cobb, Gent., John
Greenwood, for his lands and mill; Thos.
Thompson, for Harpleyes; John Blocke, for
Wynn's lands; John Emperor, Gent., for Mr.
Eacherd's; Edward Cooke, Gent.; Richard Fiske,
for Pecke's lands; the tenants of Robert Creake."

THE DRAINAGE COMMISSION.

On the drainage of the marshes this Commission
was appointed in 1799, and holds an annual
business meeting. The following have held the
office of Clerk to the Commissioners:—

1802.   Charles Francis, Farmer, Upton.
1814.   George Munford.
1818 to 1840.   Henry Codling.
1840 to 1857.   James Brown.
1857 to 1879.   Wm. Evans, S. Walsham.
1880.   Arthur W. Preston, Esq., Solicitor,
        Norwich.

The Commissioners of 1802 consisted of John
Whaites, John Holmes, William Waters, Thos.
Day, Thos. Dawson, who held their business
meetings at the Cock Inn, then kept by John
Clare, and in 1806 by Samuel Bunn.

SUBSIDY AND SHIP MONEY.

There is a subsidy roll at the Public Record
Office, "dated 4 Jany., 15 Hen. VIII.,* in response
to a grant of Parliament of 15 April preceding,
in which cvij*s*. iiij*d*. was received from the town
of Upton, Norfolk, for which John Bullock
and Christopher Browneswete were the under-
constables."

Mason, in his *History of Norfolk*, quotes the
levy of ship money, in Charles I.'s reign, in Upton,
in common with other parishes :—

LEVY OF SHIP MONEY IN 1636.

	SUMME.			THE MINISTER FOR HIS ESTATE.					
				ECCLESIASTIC.			TEMPORALL.		
	£.	*s*.	*d*.	£.	*s*.	*d*.	£.	*s*.	*d*.
Vpton...	16	17	3	- 0	4	0	- 0	0	0

The minister at that time would have been
Master Thomas More. Mason says of this ship
money :—

"It was in 1634 that the great question of
ship money arose, out of the necessity to find
funds to suppress the piratical adventurers that
frequented our coasts. Lord Bury has said that
it was 'to protect the Yarmouth fishery boats,

* 1523-4. This subsidy was, no doubt, to prosecute the war with
France, and had been reluctantly granted by Parliament.

and to keep the Dutch from our shores, that Charles and his advisers hit upon this notable expedient, which eventually cost the king his life and crown.'"

UPTON BROAD.

This is one of the least known of the Norfolk Broads, owing to its want of connection with the river. It is divided into the Great and Little Broads, the former measuring 22a. or. op., and the latter 7a. 1r. op. The carrs and the marsh-land contiguous to the Broad were, early in the century, famous as the nesting-place of the black tern, or sea swallow. The Rev. R. Lubbock, in his *Fauna of Norfolk*, says the tern "used, some years ago, to breed in myriads at Upton. The nests were placed upon the dry eminences in a very swampy part of the marshes, amongst low alders. And, in those days, they were spread, during summer, over a large extent of marsh. The fens, miles from Upton, were enlivened by blue dars, as they were always called; now months pass away without the appearance of a single bird." The Upton marshes or doles have also been known as the haunt of the bittern, the grebe, and the otter.

There is a tradition that, generations ago, Upton was a favourite resort of smugglers, who brought the contraband goods up the river Bure, and hid them in the parish. One famous hiding-place is said to have been Upton Broad, where, tradition hath it, sundry kegs of whiskey were wont to be submerged, until a suitable opportunity occurred for their disposal.

COINS.

Many coins have been found in the village from time to time, of which the following are in my possession :—Silver penny of Edward III., copper farthing of Charles I., Norfolk and Suffolk 1*s.* token, silver ; all found at the restoration of the church. An Irish ½*d.* of James II., 1691, found in a garden in the Boat Lane. This coin is one of the brass halfpence struck at Limerick by the followers of James, after he had been defeated and had escaped from Ireland ; it was called a Hibernia. The obverse shews the bust of the deposed king, and the reverse the figure of Hibernia seated, holding a cross in her right hand, while her left rests on a harp. Being found so near the probable landing-place of the smugglers, suggests the idea that probably this coin was dropped by one of them.

Coal Charity.

The sum of £200, bequeathed by the late John Waters, Esq., has been invested in Government Consols, and the interest is paid yearly to the vicar and churchwardens, to be expended in coal, to be distributed amongst those of the poor of the parish whom they may select.

CHAPTER VII.

Of Ancient Wills : Extracts of Upton Wills, from 1426 to 1762.

ALICE GYLMYN of Upton. To be buried in the cemetery of St. Margaret of Upton; to high altar there, 4*d*.; her son, Thomas Oter* of Pannisford, a bushel of barley; her sons, Tho. Hoffen and Tho. Gamyn, the same ; Ralph Thurkeld * of Upton. * Executors. Dated on the Feast of SS. Fabian and Sebastian, 1426. Proved 27th June, 1427.—Consistory Court, Register Surflete, fo. 9.

STEPHEN BERYNGTON of Upton. To be buried in the cemetery of St. Margaret there; to high altar, 12*d*.; repair of church, 2*s*.; to the light of St. Mary, 6*d*.; to light of St. Nicholas, 3*d*. ; John Gay, John Beston, John Kebyl and Margaret his wife, Edward Attwood. Thomas, testator's son, executor. Alice, wife of testator. Dated 20th June, 1435. Proved 29th June, 1435.—Consistory Court, Surflete, 177.

KATHERINE, wife of EDWARD TAYLOR of Upton. To be buried in the cemetery of St. Margaret there; John

Attewell and Margaret his wife, and Katherine their daughter; Tho. Game of Upton. Dated 9th Sept., 1435. Proved 12th Sept., 1435.—Consistory Court, Surflete, 181.

THOMAS CLERK, Chaplain of Upton. To be buried in chancel of St. Margaret there; high altar, 6s. 8d.; to light of Blessed Mary and the other lights in the said church, 2s.; repair of church, 3s. 4d.; four orders of Friars Mendicant in Norwich, 10s. in equal portions; each leper-house, 6d.; Agnes Gay, 3s. 4d.; Thos., son of Henry Pickering, 6s. 8d.; Wm. Eston, 3s. 4d.; each of my "filio et filia spirituali" (? godchildren), a bushel of malt; to fraternity of St. John de Reedys, 3s. 4d.; he directs his executors to buy an acre of arable land in Clepysby, "in auxiliam xvme dñi Regis inppm cum venit in villa de Clepysby antedo et non ad aliũ usũ." Which I understand to mean towards the fifteenths of the lord the king for ever, when it comes to the turn of that parish to contribute and to no other use—fifteenths being a well-known tax— for I don't suppose the king himself ever came to Clippesby.[1] Residue to Dominus Wm. Bisshopp, Rector of Byrlyngham, and Peter and Henry Pykering of same place, executors. Dated 24th July, 1444. Proved 4th Aug., 1444.—Reg. Wilby, fo. 49, Consistory Court.

JOHN WISSETT[2] of Upton. To be buried in churchyard of St. Margaret; to high altar, 4d.; to our Lady's light, 3d.; Alice his wife; a priest to sing for him for half a year. John Wissett his father, Tho. Andrews, executors.

---

[1] Note by Mr. T. R. Tallack.

[2] There is a Thos. Wyssett will (of Upton, 1513) in vol. i. of *Norfolk Archæological Society's Proceedings*. This Thos. Wyssett gave "to the hallowynge of the greatt bell, iiis. iiiid." His brass still in situ.

ALICE MYLLER of Upton. To be buried in the cemetery of St. Margaret there; high altar, 12*d*.; light of Blessed Mary, 12*d*.; to fabric of church, 12*d*.; residue to executors, John Poleyn and Robert Wene. Dated 16th Nov. die lune, 1449. Proved 27th Dec., 1449.—Consistory Court, Register Aleyn, fo. 34.

THOMAS GAME of Upton. To be buried in cemetery of St. Margaret there; high altar, 40*d*.; repair and emendation of church, 23*s*. 4*d*.; Matilda, wife; John Den and Beatrix his wife; Alice, daughter; Richard, son. His property was between Tho. Wyssett's on north, John Smith's on south, and abutted on lane leading to Upton Church on west. John Game of Norwich; John Game, son, and John Smith of Upton, were executors. Dated 26th Sept., 1451. Proved 10th Nov., 1451.

Consist. Admon. in Register Aleyn, 26th May, 1452. JOHN COBBE of Upton. Granted to Christian, the relict, Tho. Ewyng of S. Walsham, and Tho. Cossey of Upton.

Consist. Admon. in Register Aleyn, 14th Oct., 1456. JOHN FEN of Upton. Admon. granted to John Fen, John Wysset, and Robert Fen.

THOMAS MASSENGER of Upton. To be buried in cemetery of St. Margaret, Virgin and Martyr; high altar, 20*d*.; light of Blessed Mary, 6*d*.; repair of church, 2*s*.; to Fishley Church, 6*d*.; to guild of St. John Baptist of Upton, 4 bushels of malt; to Rachel, wife, lands, &c., which I late had of the executors of John Neve of Upton, and, after her death, same to be sold, and proceeds to find a proper priest to celebrate for his soul and that of his wife, in Upton Church. Lands said to be at Pylesmere, Blakelond (late Olive Grint's and Robert Cook's), at Fysschelehill "Subter le Intim" (*sic*) at Sparkysgap, at Massesdole, and le Fendole. John Mayn, senr., of South Walsham, John, eldest son, executors. John, youngest son, a close at Kergate and at Grovele, and a cottage called "Lombes"; Edmund, son, Joan, daughter, Agnes, daughter, land at Foxlond, next John Weybriggs; and Ellen, daughter, land at Tho. Dering's gate and at Wullestubbe. Dated 5th Feb., 1459. Proved 8th March, 1459.—Consistory Court, Brosiard, fo. 181.

JOHN TAYLOR of Upton, the elder. To be buried in cemetery of St. Margaret there; high altar, 6d.; light of Blessed Mary, 6d.; repair of church, 4 bushels of malt; Friars Minors of Norwich, 3s. 4d.; John, son; Robert Bemond and his wife Margaret, my daughter. Walter Brend and Wm. Andrew of Upton, executors. Dated 1462 (no day). Proved 28th May, 1462.—Consistory Court, Brosiard, fo. 285.

JOHN WEYBRIGGE of Upton. To be buried in cemetery of St. Margaret there; high altar, 2s.; light of Blessed Mary, 20d.; emendation of church and repair of walls of the cemetery, 6s. 8d.; Beatrice, daughter; John Dawys, son-in-law; Agnes, daughter; Margaret, daughter; William, son, land held of the manors of Upton, Acle, South Walsham, and Randworth, and, at his death, if no issue, to be sold, and proceeds to celebrate masses, repair ways and bridge of Weybrigg, and other pious uses; Felix, wife, land called "Broodes" at Hangyngwong, near land of the lord of Upton on the west, land at Harefen and Westakynheld, close called "Kergatesyerd"; John, son, to celebrate for his soul. Tho. Archer, William, son, executors. Church of Holy Trinity of Norwich. He directs his son John, whom he calls "monachum filium meum" to be his supervisor, by licence of his abbot. Dated 1st April, 1465. Proved 20th July, 1465.—Consistory Court, Brosiard, fo. 358.

JOHN GOTE of Upton. To be buried in the cemetery of St. Margaret; high altar, 3s. 4d.; light of St. Mary, 10d.;

repair of church, 13s. 4d.; guild of St. Margaret in the said church, 4 bush. malt; guild of St. Mary's in the said church, 2 bush. malt; Friars Minors of Norwich to pray for him, 4 bush. malt; to church of St. Edmund, King and Martyr, at Thurne, 6s. 8d. Robert, brother; Alice, wife; Robert, father; Robert Wynne, executors. Edward, son; Robert, son; Cecily, dau.; Agnes, dau. Dated 8th Sept., 1465. Proved 10th Nov., 1465.—Consistory Court, Cobald, 51.

HENRY DERSHAM of Upton. To be buried in cemetery of St. Margaret; high altar, 12d.; light of Blessed Mary, 8d.; repair of church for my sepulchre (? not clear); repair of way in Hobbysgate, 6s. 8d. Joan, sister; Rose Peper, John Bornham, Wm. Bornham. Walter Brond, Tho. Peper, executors. Jno. Brond, Elen Brond, Adam Dersham, and Joan his wife, Henry Dersham, Jno. Pepyr. Dated in die S. Dionisii & Sociorum ejus, 1465. Proved 14th Oct., 1465. —Consistory Court, Cobald, 71.

GEOFFREY KAN of Upton. (Cf. Geoffrey Can de Upton, almost duplicate copy, yet dates of month different). To be buried in the cemetery of St. Margaret's church; to high altar, 3s. 4d.; to light of St. Mary, 6d.; to emendation and reparation of church, 13s. 4d.; 20s. to poor of Upton and adjacent parishes. Alice Camplyon, John Goot, and Ralph Dunmowe, executors. Witnessed at Upton on festival of St. Lawrence, Martyr, 1465, by John Messenger, senr., Wm. Methwold, Robt. Bemond, John Talyour, Wm. Wynn, Wm. Andrew, Robt. Couper, and others. Proved 27th Sept., 1465.—Consistory Court, Jekkys, 5.

EDWARD FOWLAND of Upton. To be buried in the cemetery of St. Margaret; to high altar, 12d.; light of Blessed Mary, 6d.; repair of the church, 3s. 4d.; Stephen, brother, land which was my father John's, near the north marsh. Cecily, sister. A priest to celebrate for him; Henry Mounfort of S. Walsham, and his brother, Stephen Fowland, executors. Dated 4th Sept., 1465. Proved 28th Sept., 1465. Geoff. Methwold, John Carter, and John Den, witnesses.—Consistory Court, Cobald, fo. 22.

GEOFFREY CAN de Upton. To be buried in cemetery of St. Margaret; to high altar, 3*s.* 4*d.*; to light of St. Mary, 6*d.*; repair of church, 13*s.* 4*d.*; to poor, &c., &c. Alice Camplyon; John Gote and Ralph Dunmowe, executors. Robert Cowper, Jno. Messenger, senr., Wm. Methwold, Robt. Bemond, Jno. Talyur, Wm. Wyn, Wm. Andrew, witnesses. Dated at Upton, 1465, on the feast of St. Lawrence. Proved 10th Nov. 1465.—Consistory Court, Cobald, fo. 51.

JOHN MESSENGER of Upton, the younger. To be buried in cemetery of St. Margaret; high altar, 12*d.*; to light of St. Mary, 6*d.*; Katherine, wife, my close in Kergate and at Grovele, cottage called Lombys, which my father Thomas gave me by will. Edward Skoteman, Vicar of Upton; Katherine, wife; Tho. Keryng, executors. Dated· die lune prox. post festum S. Bartholom., Apl. 1465, Monday after S. Bartholomew. Proved 9th Nov. 1465. — Consistory Court, Cobald, fo. 50.

JOAN ANDREW, Widow, of Upton. To be buried in cemetery of St. Margaret; high altar, 6*d.*; light of St. Mary, 4*d.*; repair of church, 12*d.*; tenement called "le Meysters." Henry, son; Tho. Peper, executors. Dated on day of Decollation of St. Jno. Baptist, 1465. Proved 14th Oct. 1465.—Consistory Court, Cobald, fo. 71.

JOHN SMYTH of Upton. To be buried in cemetery of St. Margaret's Church; high altar, 20*d.*; light of Blessed Mary, 12*d.*; to repair of the church, 20*s.*; to Friars Preachers of Norwich; repair of bridge at Weybrigg, 4 bushels of barley; 7 acres of free land, which were Edward my father's land at

Grovele called Ranenysacr, Rowesdole, longhalfacr called Domysday, Gerards hedstyk; a priest to celebrate for him in Upton Church for a year; Beatrice Brown, dau., to have Hangingwonge, land called Curfefeu, which was John Taylor's; lands called Wetyswonge, Cleylond, Oldgate, land near Agnes Barker's; Margaret, wife, messuage in Upton and land held of the Bishop and the manor of Fishele. Robert Wyn, John Ronde, executors. Dated on the feast of St. Peter ad vincula, 1466. Proved 19th Oct. 1466.

THOMAS WYCETE of Upton. To be buried in the church of St. Margaret, before the high altar of the blessed Thomas the Martyr; to the "gardianis sive custodibus bonorum ejusdam ecclesie" for my sepulchre, 6s. 8d.; to high altar of St. Margaret, 3s. 4d.; to fabric and repair of church, " Itm. lego ad fabriciam sive ad repacōnem eccłie pāce ut pochiani eiusdem aiãm meam in oracionibȝ suis pēant in recomendat," 13s. 4d., i.e., that the parishioners may remember to pray for his soul in their prayers; to the increment of the light before the image of the Blessed Mary in said church, 2s.; 13s. 4d. to the Abbot and Convent of St. Benedict de Hulmo to pray for him; to the lepers at Norwich and Yarmouth, friars there, &c.; to brother John Belaw of Friars Minors of Norwich for a trental of St. Gregory, 10s.; executors to pay 23s. 4d. for repairing the cope to be used in the said church of St. Margaret; Isabel, wife of John Elger, citizen and goldsmith of Norwich, and Margaret their daughter; each of his godchildren; all my lands, late held of Edmund Wychyngham, lord of Upton; John, son; Thomas, son of said John; Margaret and Helen, daughters; priest to sing for him in Upton Church for a year. Wm. Wynn of Upton, Jno. Elger of Norwich, son John, executors. Dated 3rd Jan. 1467. Proved 14th Feb. 1467.—Consistory Court, Jekkys, fo. 92.

THOS. DERYNG, senr., of Upton. To guild of St. John
Baptist there.—P. 101, MS. penes W. Rye.

ROBERT ANDREW of Upton. To be buried in cemetery
of St. Margaret, Virgin and Martyr; to high altar, 20*d.*;
to light of St. Mary, 8*d.*; to fabric of the church, 6*s.* 8*d.*;
Thomas, " my brother, 3*s.* 4*d.*, to celebrate for my soul, and
for a 'certain'* for four years after my death "; Joan, wife,
to have a chamber on the east side, next the field gate,
called "nova camera," in my house at Upton. Thomas,
son, and John Wissett, executors. Dated 12th Oct. 1469.
Proved 30th Oct. 1469.—Consistory, Brosiard, fo. 167.

FELICIA WEYBRYG, widow. To be buried in cemetery
of St. Margaret, Virgin and Martyr, of Upton ; to high
altar, 2*s.* ; pro uno panno pendente coram eodem sum. altar.
in tempore quadrageso ; to light of Blessed Mary there, 4*d.* ;
two trentals of St. Gregory, Papa, to be celebrated—one for
my soul, and one for soul of John Weybryg, our parents
and friends,—for which, 20*s.* ; to poor of Upton, 6*s.* 8*d.*
(This will is not finished in the register). Dated 10th Feb.
1473. There is a note that a fee was excused, propter
exilitatem bonorum.—Consistory, Reg. Gelour, fo. 72.

JOHN COSSEY of Upton. To be buried in cemetery of St.
Margaret there ; to high altar, 20*d.* ; to sustentation of Gild
of St. Jno. Baptist in eadem, 2*s.*; to repair of said church,
20*s.* ; Elen Norwich, my mother, 20*s.* ; Ric. Walle, 2*s.* ;
Ric. Umfrey de Metyngham, 2*s.*; Agnes, sister; " ad
peregrinand p me usꝗ ad capell ƀte M'e de Walsingham,"
20*s.* and one blanket ; Nicholas and Thomas, brothers, and
Agnes, sister, to have sixteen sheep and six lambs; a secular

---

* Blomefield, under South Walsham, says : " Alice Carre, widow,
in 1523, the profits of four acres of land here to keep a *certeyn* for
her and her friends."—See also will of John Fenn.·

I 2

priest to sing for a year for him in Upton, and to have 8*s.* 4*d.*
Speaks of lands he had of Thomas Cossey, his father.
Nic. Cossey, Wm. Wyn, executors. Dated 3rd April, 1472.
Proved 30th April, 1473.—Consistory, Reg. Paynot, fo. 5.

JOHN FENN of Upton. To be buried in the cemetery of
the church of St. Margaret; to high altar there, 8*d.*; to light of
St. Mary Virgin, 4*d.*; Robert, son, and Robert Fenn, brother,
to have his tenements, " et omĩa que teneo in bondagio de
Ducissa Norf. in villa et teritorio de Upton et Walsham,"
which he had surrendered to Richd. Southwell and —
de Bokenham, Esqs.; after the death of Letice his wife
he desires "un. cert. vulgariter nuncup. a certane" to be
celebrated for them, their parents, friends, and benefactors,
in Upton church for two and a half years; Cecily, dau., 40*s.*;
Robert, son, all his freeholds in Upton. Robert, son, and
Robert, brother, executors. Dated 13th July, 1474. Proved
27th Oct. 1474, by executors.—Consistory, Reg. Gelour,
fo. 75.

JOHN ATHOW, SEN., of Upton. To be buried in cemetery of St. Margaret, Virg. and Mart., de Upton; to high
altar there, 12*d.*; to light of Blessed Mary, Virgin, in same,
8*d.*; Blide, wife, two acres of arable land, apud Habenes-
gate in Fyshele; John, son, and his sisters; Thomas,
brother. John Thurkyld of Wyckhampton, Rob. Eston of
Upton, Blide, wife, executors. Rob. Dockyng, Ric. Oky,
Jno. Godewyn, witnesses. Dated " die d'nica prox. ant.
fest. S^d Andreæ, Ap'li," 1479. Proved at Hemblyngton by
wife and Thurkyld, but no date given.—Consistory, Reg.
Aubrey, fo. 44.

NICHOLAS COSSEY of Upton. To be buried in cemetery
of St. Margaret there; high altar, 4*s.*; light of Blessed
Mary, 16*d.*: repair of the image and tabernacle of St.
Nicholas, Bishop, in same church, 40*s.*; priest to celebrate

for him for a year, and preferably brother John Yarmouth, if he will; Agnes, wife; Richard, son; Ellen, mother; Thomas, son; Nicholas Edwards of Upton to have lands, called "Bardolf," in South Walsham; "Hesylgrave in Upton" named; Thomas, my late brother. William Wynn, Richard Baker of Stokesby, Thomas Andrews of Upton, executors. Dated die Sabbati prox. ante fest. S. Mich⁵ Archangel, 1479. Proved 7th Oct. 1479.—Consistory, Reg. Newbrye, fo. 8.

JOHN WISSETT of Upton. To be buried in churchyard of St. Margaret there; to high altar, 4d.; to our Lady's light, 3d.; Alice, wife; Robert Iryng; a priest to sing half a year in Upton Church for his soul. John Wissett "his fader," and Tho. Andrewes, executors. Dated 11th Oct. 1479. Proved 2nd Nov. 1479.—Consistory, Reg. Audry, fo. 17.

PETER ERLE of Upton, 1487.—P. 116, MS. penes W. Rye.

THO. ANDREWS of Upton. My body to be buryed before the pyktur of our lady in the south syde of the Chirche of Seynt Margrette, virgyn and martyr, of Upton foreseyd. To our lady lyght in the seyd Chirche, xijd.; to the repacōn of the seyd chirche for my burying space, vjs. viijd. Dated 20th Sept. 1498 (? 1488). Proved 19th Oct. 1488 (*sic*).— *Norf. Arch.*, from L'Estrange's will notes, penes W. Rye.

MARGT. MASSINGER of Upton, widow, 1490. Lights of B.V.M., St. John Baptist, St. Margaret.—P. 140, MS. penes W. Rye.

ROGER TAYLOR of Upton. To be buried in churchyard of St. Margaret, Virg. and Martyr, of Upton; high altar in said church, 12d.; our Lady's light in same, 12d.; repair of said church, 3s. 4d.; every householder in Upton, 1d.; every person not housled in said parish, bread value ½d.; Austin Freers of Southtown, 12d.; White Freers of Norwich, 12*d.*; Grey Freers of Norwich, 12*d.*; Black Freers of Norwich, 12*d.*; Agnes Amys, dau., messuage I purchased of Tho. Daured, for her life, and then to Thos. Amys her son (paying dues to the lord thereof); said Agnes, dau., a posnett of brass; Wm., son, household stuff; Katherine Taylor, daughter of Wm. Taylor; £4 for a cloth with the frenge for the high awter in the said church of St. Margaret of Upton, when it may arise from my debts. Wm. Wyne and Jno. Taylor, executors, 3*s.* 4*d.* each. Dated 5th Oct. 1492. Proved 21st Nov. 1492.—Consistory, Reg. Aubry, fo. 118.

JOHN BENSELYN of Upton, 12th Sept., 1499. Our Lady's light; reparation of the bells, 23*s.* 4*d.*—P. 314, MS. penes W. Rye.

THOMAS MESSYNGER of Upton. To be buried in church-yard of St. Margaret; to high altar, 12*d.*; to our Lady's light, 12*d.*; to repair of church there, 3*s.* 4*d.* Robert, brother, and Roger Davy, bro.-in-law; executors. Dated on Thursday before St. Andrew, Apostle, 1504. Proved 4th Jany. 150$\frac{4}{5}$.—Consistory Court, Rix, fo. 53.

WILLIAM WYNNE of Upton. To be buried in church of St. Margaret of Upton, in the myde ally, and a gravestone to be laid over him of the price of 26*s.* 8*d.*; to high altar, 13*s.* 4*d.*; to our Lady's light in same church, 40*d.*; to paynting and gilding of the tabernacle of St. Nicholas in the same church, 6*s.* 8*d.*; to the guild of St. Peter, 6*s.* 8*d.*, on condition that the brethren and sistern will begin the guild and uphold it; repair of Weybrigge and the caunsy; to stoning the church of Upton 20 marcs, and more if it need; a secular priest to sing in Upton Church for him and his friends; his houses, called "Jebbes" and "Deyes," in Upton; Agnes, wife, sole executrix; Willm. Gotte, godson, my messuage, where I dwell, cleped "Wycely's" and the next thereto, cleped "Chapman's"; land at Sparkesgap; messuage called "Miller's"; close at the town's end called "Sike Silver's" and "Snethes"; mill, late John Peper's; land at Brandesdele, late Willm. Brother's; land at Foxlane, Pylesmere, Hangyngwong, Greneshedstok, Pottbrede, Stakenhill; land at close end which I hold of the Bishop of Norwich; Richard, son; Ellen, daughter; Thomas, son; Ralf, son; Robert, son; Alice, daughter; Elizabeth Chapman, "my nese." Mr. Felmyngham, of Ranworth, supervisor. Dated 25th Oct. 1505. Proved 18th Nov. 1505.—Consistory, Reg. Rix, fo. 232.

AGNES WYNN of Upton, widow. To be buried in church of St. Margaret, "in the middle aley before the chancel dore" (? screen door); to high altar, 6s. 8d.; to our Lady's light, 20d.; Richard, son; Alice, daughter; William, son; Thomas, son; Elyn, daughter; Raf, son; Wm. Goote; Elizabeth Chapman; 1d. to every man and woman who are howslynges in Upton, and every child four fardyng loaves or two value a peny; a priest to sing for her and her husband for a year; her executors to sell her messuage, late Dokkynge's, and her ground, late Amy Rogers', where Wm. Brownstrete lives. Mr. Francis Southwell, Esquire, Richard, her son, and Tho. Gylberd of North Burlingham, executors. Dated St. Katherine's Day, 1505. Proved 25th April, 1506.—Consistory Court, Rix, fo. 333.

MARGT. BEAMOND of Upton, widow, 1507. To every house of friars in Norwich and Southtown whereof I am sister, 12d.—P. 348, MS. penes W. Rye.

JOHN CATON of Upton. To be buried in the churchyard of Upton, by his father and mother; to high altar, 3s. 4d.; to repair of church, 6s. 8d.; to light of our Lady, 20d.; every order of Freres in Norwich, four bushels barley; to Freres Austin of Southtown, four bushels barley; to every house of

sick folk at Norwich gates, 4*d.*; his messuage in Upton to
be sold, and a secular priest to be provided out of proceeds
to sing for a year for him in Upton Church; and another
priest for his father and mother and all good friends for
three-quarters of a year; to every priest on his burying day,
4*d.*; and every clerk, 2*d.*; to every man, woman, and child
then, 1*d.*; Agnes Toppes, "my suster"; Jno. Cann, godson;
Margaret Fenn, "suster," a cow each; Tho. Symonds, four
bushels of barley; Agnes Symonds, sen., two bushels of
barley; Isbel Gybbes, a cow; Margaret Vyn, godchild, four
bushels of barley; Isbel, wife, lands in Postwick. John
Cowper, executor. Syr Tho. Gresmer, vicker of Upton,
Robert Reynes of Acle, with other, witnesses. Dated 31st
Aug. 1508. Proved 28th Oct. 1508.—Consistory, Reg.
Spiltymbre, fo. 110.

WILLIAM BRONSTRETE of Upton. To be buried in
churchyard of St. Margaret, Virgin, there; to high awter
there, 10*d.*; to our Lady's light in same, 6*d.*; to repair
of said church, 20*d.*; to house of White Friars in Norwich,
12*d.*; Margaret, wife, messuage where I dwell for her life,
and then same to be sold and proceeds divided between
Elyn Bronstrète, John Bronstrete, Robert Bronstrete, and
Stephen Bronstrete, his children. Margaret, wife, Christopher and Wm. Bronstrete, executors. Dated 26th Dec.
1509. Proved 21st Jan. 1510.—Consistory, Reg. Johnson,
fo. 9.

THOMAS GRESMER, vicar' perpetuus de Upton. To be
buried "in cancello coram ymagine St* Margaretæ," to
which he gives an embroidered "kercher" and a new
vestment "de le velvet"; to repair of church, 6*s.* 8*d.*;
to light of Blessed Mary, 12*d.*; to each house of Friars
in Norwich, 10*s.*; a trental to be sung in each for him;
each house of lepers in Norwich, 12*d.*; to the mother

church of Norwich, 6s. 8d.; "my poor parishes" to have
between them "mea grana, viz., ordeum, brasium, &
avena"; T. Wiset, 8d., and his wife, 4d.; each parishioner,
1d.; each child, ½d.; Rob. Bensley, 12d., and his wife, 4d.;
John Taylor, 4d., and his wife, 2d.; Acle Church, a coomb
of malt; Boughton Church, ditto; Walsham Church, ditto;
Havergate Church, ditto; Fishle Church, ditto; Prior of
Weybrig for repair of Priory, 40d.; fabric of St. Cuthbert's
Church, 10s.; each priest at his obsequies, 4d.; each curate,
8d.; each clerk, 2d. John Curat, notary, executor. Dated
15th April, 1511. Proved 23rd Aug. 1511.—Consistory,
Reg. Johnson, fo. 65.

ROBERT BENSLYN of Upton. To be buried before the
quere dore of church of St. Margaret there; to high altar,
3s. 4d.; to light of our Lady there, 2s.; to perk light in
same, 2s.; repair of same church, 13s. 4d.; to the church
where my body is buried, "a honest vestment and that
longing therto, the color wight damask, to the value of four
pounds thirteen shillings and fourpence"; to edification of
stepull of St. Lawrence in S. Walsham, 6s. 8d.; to high altar
of Fishly, 6d.; to repair of same church, 12d.; to repair of
church of Ranworth, 3s. 4d.; twenty masses to be sung at
Scala Celi in Westmynster for him and his friends; a priest
to pray for him for a year where he is buried; to White,
Black, and Grey Freres in Norwich, and Austen Freres in
Southtown, 6s. 8d. equally; I will my Lord Abbot of St.
Benet to have 12d.; to the Prior, 12d.; and to iche monk,
4d.; each house of sekemen at gates of Norwich, 12d.;
Beatrice, wife, my place and lands that were John Barker's,
place, &c., in S. Walsham I bought of Jno. Greene, till his
son Robert is sixteen years of age; Alis, dau., tenement
bought of Nicholas Sadd; tenement called Branches to be
sold; each of his godchildren, four bushels of barley. Wife

and son Robert, executors. Christopher Speyn, supervisor, and to have 13s. 4d. for his labour. Dated 24th Sept. 1515. Proved 7th Feby. 151⅚.—Consistory, Reg. Spyrling, fo. 172.

THOMAS TAYLOR of Upton. To be buried in the churchyard of St. Margaret there; to the high altar, 2s. : to our Lady's light, 12d.; to the pearke light, 12d.; to repair of the church, 3s. 4d.; to four orders of Freers, a coombe of barley each; to every lazar house in Norwich, 4d.; a placebo & direge & mass of requiem at burial, to every priest there, 4d., and every clerk, 2d.; to every child "yᵗ canne sey De profundis," 1d.; every man, woman, and child to have on that day, ½d., "in bred to pray for my soule"; Agnes, wife, to have tenement in Upton called Bemonds ; eldest dau., a calf; Austin Freers, at Southtown, at scala celi, thirty masses. Robert Wells and the wife, executor and executrix. Ed. Wytherley, Beatrix Wrightson, witnesses. 12th Feb. 1517. No proof in register.—Consistory, Palgrave, fo. 234.

RICHARD PETID of Upton. To be buried in churchyard of St. Margaret of Upton ; to high altar, 4d.; to repair of said church, 6d.; to light of our Lady, 4d.; Johan, wife, sole executrix, messuage called Masengers that late Robert Petid had by exchange of John Jamis. Dated 12th May, 1522. Proved 12th July, 1522, by executrix.—Consistory, Reg. Alablaster, fo. 146.

RAFE WYN of Upton. To be buried in churchyard there ; to high altar there, 16d.; to perk light in eadem ecclᵃ, 6d.; to houses of "lacers" at Norwich and Yarmouth, 6d. each ; five masses of five wounds to be sung at his burial ; six loads of gravel from Myhilborow hill to be laid in the ways of Upton at his exors. discretion; Agnes, wife, cattle and household goods; John, son; Robt. Wyn. son; Joan Wyn, daughter ; Agnes, daughter; Christr. Wyn, son; John the son to manage property, "but if it happen the said John my son be taken to serve the King's Majesty in his wars, before the feast of St. Faith the Virgin next ensuing, and doth not come back before the feast of All Saints next following," wife to manage; a trental to be sung in Upton Church for him; Thomas, brother. Agnes, the wife, and Richard Wyn, the brother, exors. Sir Edmund Taylor, Jno. Ramsey, Wm. Gymyngham, Edmd. Gap, Jno. Speyn, Christr. Speyn, Edmd. Flower, witnesses. Dated 14th Feb. 1544. Proved 14th March, 1544.—Consistory, Reg. Puntyng, fo. 220.

RICHARD WYNN of Upton. To be buried in church or churchyard of Upton; to high altar of Upton, 3s. 4d.; to the perkelight, four bushels of malt and two of wheat; "to yᵉ mendyng and repation of Upton stepul when yᵉ townshype gothe aboute ye repation and mendyng of yᵉ same steypll, 40s."; each house of lasers at yᵉ gates of Norwich, 12d.; each house of lasers at yᵉ gates of Yarmouth, 12d.; Alice, wife; Robert, son, land I bought of Andriou Preston, and my tenement in Acle market; Rafe, son, 38 marks; Thomasyn and Elizabeth, daus., 40s. each; William Tymp; Tho. Curteys, servant, 3s. 4d.; Jno. Brown, servant, 12d.; Jone Hexam, servant, 12d.; Alice Rayner, servant, 12d.; John Martens, late my servant, 40d.; Gregorie Goot, godchild, 12d.; Steven Goot, godchild, 12d.; each other godchild, 12d.; Richard, son of Robert Vyn, 20s.; Elizabeth, dau. of Robert Vyn, 20s.; thirty masses to be sung for him; to repair of Wyckhampton Church, 6s. 8d.; to Veker of Halvergate, 6s. 8d.; to repair of Halvergate Church, 13s. 4d.; to repair of Fishley Church, 12d. Christr. Spen and wife Alice, executors. Wm. Moreson, Jno. Speyn, Jno. Ramsey, Edmd. Taylor, and other, witnesses. Dated in the year 1546 (no day). No proof, but 1549-50 book.— Consistory, Reg. Welman, 1st part, fo. 21.

JOHN PODDES of Fishley. To repair of Upton steeple, 6s. 8d.; church of Fishley, 3s. 4d.; to be buried in the church of St. Edmund of Acle. Dated 10th March, 1545. Proved 16th May, 1546.

JOHN DURRANT of Upton, husbandman. To be buried in sanctuary of St. Margaret of Upton; to said church, 8d.; to poor there, 14d.; Betres Bell, Harry Crastwell, John Taylor, senr., Mawte, wife; Elizabeth, daughter. William, son, executor. John, son. Wm. Gymyngham, Edmd. Cappes, John Baker, John Morwyn, witnesses. Dated 31st Augt. 1551. Proved 17th Jany. 1554.—Norwich Archdeaconry, fo. 245.

11th May, 1555. Robert Wheatlye, deceased. Admon. granted to Elizabeth his relict.—Consistorial Act Bk., Nor.

WILLIAM REDE of Upton. To be buried in churchyard of St. Margaret; high altar of Thyrne; repair of Upton Church, 3s. 4d.; five masses of five wounds of our Lord to be sung in Upton Church for him; priest to sing for half a year for him. Elynor, wife, John, son, executors. Property in Thirne, Ashby, and Oby; godchildren, 4d. each; Nic. Pibottell; Amy Fraree, servant. Roger Rokwood, Esqre., John Rede the elder, Wm. Southgate, Wm. Moreson, witnesses. Dated 12th April, 1547. Proved 8th Octr. 1555.—Norwich Archdeaconry, 1555, fo. 321.

AGNES BRAYE of Upton. Admon. granted by Consistory Court, 24th May, 1557, to William Turnor of Ocle, her son.—In Consistory Admon. Book, No. 2, fo. 206.

ROBERT WYNNE of Upton. To be buried in the churchyard of Upton; to high altar in the said church, 6d.; Amie, wife, lands in Upton and S. Walsham for her life, and then to William, son, he to pay his two sisters, Elizabeth and Alys, £10 each. Richd. Taylor, supervisor. Wife, executrix. Jno. Bales, John Bubbinge, John Morwyn, Rob.

Moneyman, and others, witnesses. Dated 14th May, 1559.
Proved 19th June, 1559, by widow.—Consistory, Reg.
Colman, fo. 417.

WILLIAM TYMPE of Upton, yeoman. To be buried in
churchyard there; to poor men's box of said town, 12d.;
Jno. Fyster's children, 4d. amongst them equally; Cecely,
wife, copyholds for her life, and then to Elizabeth, daughter;
Raffe Wynn, my brother; John Spanye of Oulton; John
Browne of Upton; speaks of his children. Wife, sole
executrix. Tho. Norwich, Peter Downhill, Rafe Wynn,
Richd. Smyth, Will. Reader, witnesses. Dated 26th June,
1569. Proved 26th July, 1569.—Consistory, Reg. Ponder,
fo. 205.

JOHN GAPPE of Upton, husbandman. To be buried in
churchyard there; to repair of church, 12d.; to poor of
Upton, 12d.; to Vicar of Upton, 12d.; Alice, wife, executrix;
Elizth., daughter; sister Elizabeth Sendall; nevewe Jno.
Sendall; godson Jno. Fisher; nevewe Edmd. Gappe; nece
Amy Gappe; more to poor of Upton, 3s. 9d. Rd. Taylor,
Jno. Wynne, Edw. Hilkon, witnesses. Dated 7th May, 1574.
Proved 18th Oct. 1574.—Norwich Archdeaconry, reg. 1574,
fo. 279.

1575, 28th January, Consistory. JOHN GOTE of Upton.
Admon. granted to Elizabeth his relict.

JNO. WHETLEY, husbandman, of Upton. To be buried in
churchyard of Upton; to repair of church, 12d.; to poor
men's box, 12d.; Jone, wife, sole executrix; Ellen Brownstret,
wife's daughter; Robert Whetley, brother; Alice Whetley,
sister; Gilyson Williamsonne, aunt; Lucie Clarke; Robert
Fisher, servant; Edmd. Taylor, Christopher Bullocke, Jno.
Benslynge, writer, witnesses. Dated 27th Oct. 1575. Proved
1st Decr. 1575.—Norwich Register, 1575, fo. 374.

ROBERT GREENWOOD of Upton, husbandman. To be

buried in churchyard there; Margaret, wife, executrix; John, eldest son, when 21; Hugh, son; Em., daughter; Christopher Bullock. Christr. Athowe of Upton, executor, if the wife die. 5*s.* to poor at his funeral; property in Upton, Walsham, and Fishley. Dated 7th March, 1586. Proved 20th March, 1586.—Norwich Archdeaconry, 1586, fo. 336.

RICHARD TAYLOR of Upton, yeoman. To be buried in churchyard there, near Roger Taylor, my uncle; to repair of church, 20*s.*; £4 of good English money *towards the buildinge uppe of the steeple againe*, to be paid when the parishioners doe builde upp the same; Thomas Dyerton, vicar of Upton, 20*d.*; each pore household, ·12*d.*; £5 to poor; legacies to prisoners, sick-houses, &c.; to Elizabeth, wife, my tenement sometime John Taylor's, land sometime Robert Flower's, land sometime Christr. Bromstreete, Balles yard, and Ewyn's, the Turbarye in New skore, tenement in Hobesgate Street, land on west of Upton Church, Cargate Green, Foxholes sometime Gabriel Benslinge's. Robert Taylor, my nephew, and Wm. his son; Elizabeth Taylor and Thomasine Taylor, daughters of Robert Taylor, mason; Edmund Taylor of Halvergate, senr.; Lome's two children, which he had by Alice Taylor, his wife; John, brother of Robert Taylor; Adam Taylor, nephew, Gose's tenement; Audrey, Lucy, and Margaret Taylor, children of Edmd. Taylor of Halvergate; Philip Taylor, Thomas Taylor, and Robert Taylor, nephews. Tho. Greene of North Burlingham and Hew Cooper of Upton, executors. Dated 6th July, 1587. Proved 28th June, 1588. —Norwich Archdeaconry, Liber James, 1588-9, fo. 73.

JOHN HOLTE of Upton. To be buried in churchyard there; Robert, eldest son, to have the tenement testator inhabited in Upton, when twenty-five, paying his brother John, younger son, £4; if both his sons die then his

property to go to Christopher Athowe of Upton, and
Edmunde Wynn of Upton, whom he desires to bring up
his said children, and to be executors of his will. Robert
Hannor, Tho. Browen, Tho. Dyerton, clerk, and others,
witnesses. Dated 12th Mar. 1590. Proved 8th Mar.
1591.—Consistory, Reg. Andrewes, fo. 211.

CHRISTOPHER BULLOCKE of Upton, husbandman. To be
buried in churchyard of Upton; to repair of said church,
10s.; Thomas Bullocke, youngest son; Olive Bullocke,
widow. John, eldest son, Isabel, wife, executors. Robert,
son; Margaret, daughter, wife of Robert Fosdick, and
their son Christopher. Dated 10th June, 1591. Proved
28th June, 1591.—Norwich Archdeaconry, 1591, fo. 367.

OLIFE BULLOCK of Upton, widow. To be buried in
churchyard there; to Upton parish, 3s. 4d.; Olyffe Dennys,
dau. of Nics. Dennys; Elizth. Dennys, dau. of Nics.
Dennys. Olyff Durrant, dau. of Edmond Durrant, granddau., to be executrix. Dated 26th June, 1595. Proved 16th
Augt. 1595.—Norwich Archdeaconry, fo. 298.

KATHERINE BROWNE of Upton, widow. Christopher,
son; Anthony, son; Margaret, dau., wife of Wm. Wynne;
Joan, dau., wife of John Driver; Jno. Brown, son of
Christopher; Ellen Brown, dau. of Christopher; Robert
Wynne, son of William; Rebecca Wynne, dau. of William;
Eliz. Browne, dau. of Edmund Browne; Edmond, son;
Elizabeth, Agnes, and Katherine Wynne; Amy and Margaret
Wynne; Wm., son of Christopher Browne; Robert Browne;
Margaret, wife of William Wynne; sons Christopher and
Wm. Wynne, executors. Wm. Martens of Bastwick Flegg,
supervisor. Dated 4th August, 36th Elizth. Proved 21st
Feb. 1596.—Norwich Archdeaconry.

EDMOND BROWNE of Upton, gent. Rebecca, wife (sole
executrix), freehold house where I dwell, and other my

messuages, sometime Christr. Ramsey's and Rob. Flower's, which my father John bought of them, in Upton, Fishley, Acle, Burlingham, and S. Walsham; for education of my three children, Elizth., Judith, and Martha, till Martha (youngest) be twenty-one; to repair of church, to church-wardens, 20*s.*; to poor at my burial, 20*s.*; Jelyon Walker, my maid, 10*s.* when she is twenty-one; Willm. Clark, my manservant, 20*s.*; Edmond Browne, sen., of Upton, 5*s.*; Henry Skarburgh of N. Walsham, gent., supervisor, 30*s.* Edw. Chamberlain, Jno. Baker, Ambrose Clark, witnesses. Dated 5th Mar. 45th Elizth.   Proved 23rd Mar. 1602, by executrix.—Norwich, 1602, fo. 128.

WILLIAM CYBOLE of Upton, husbandman.   To be buried in churchyard there; William, Raphe, John, sons; Elizth. Cybole, daughter; Mary Cybole, another daughter, a cow each; Robert, son, £3; Awdry, dau., wife of John Tyles of Yarmouth, 20*s.* Elizth, wife, sole executrix. Christopher Goet, Philip Taylor, Tho. Dyerton, clerk, witnesses. Dated 5th Aug., 1603.   Proved 1st Sept. 1603, by executrix.—Norwich Archd., 1603, fo. 171.

THOMAS CAPPS of Upton.   To be buried in churchyard of Upton; to repair of said church, 12*d.*; Ellen, dau., wife of Robert Fisher, houses in Upton for life, and then to Agnes Fisher, her dau., my grandchild.   Robert Fisher, son-in-law, executor.   Mary Fisher, granddau.; Katherine Fisher, granddau.; Gabriel Fisher, grandson, 40*s.*; widow Clark the younger, 4*d.*; Ame Flower, widow, 2*d.*   He surrendered his lands to Phillip Taylor, in presence of Tho. Cornwell and Jno. Barker.   Dated 27th June, 1605. Proved 6th May, 1606.—Norwich Archdy., 1606, fo. 24.

JOHN WYN of Upton, yeoman.   To be buried in church porch of Upton; to parish church of Upton, 3*s.* 4*d.*; Edward, son, houses and lands.   John, son, houses and £100;

Richard, son, houses and £40; executors. Son Edward's children, 10s. each; cousin Raphe Welles, his two children, 3s. 4d. each; John Wynn and Tho. Wynn of Norwich, 10s. each; Eliz. Howitt and each godchild, 2s.; poor of Upton, six bushels of wheat to be ground and baked into bread at his burial; also two barrels of good beer "and a penny coal"; mentions his land bought of Wilson in S. Walsham, and of John Hill in Burlingham; land between the enclosure of Christopher Goate on the south, and of the Vicar of Upton on the north; "tenement where I dwell at Cranscore." Tho. Steygould, Jno. Bensling, Gregory Goate, Antho. Browne, witnesses. Dated 9thMarch, 1605. Proved 8th Jany. 1607.—Consistory, Reg. Rowland, fo. 203.

2nd Feb. 1609. ADAM TAYLOR, deceased. Administration granted to Thomazine Taylor and Judith, wife of William Goate, daughters of the deceased, intestate.—Consist. Act Bk., Norw., 1604 to 1625.

WILLIAM WYNN of Upton, yeoman. To be buried in the churchyard there near his father; to repair of the church, 6s. 8d.; to poor of Upton, 10s. Margaret, wife, to be sole executrix, and have his lands in Upton, Fishley, Acle, Burlingham, and South Walsham for her life, and to bring up children: after her to go to Robert, son. Anthony, Edward, William, and Thomas, my four younger sons, £40 each; Margaret Wynn, Rebecca Wynn, my youngest daus., £40 each. Brother-in-law Robt. Browne of S. Walsham, yeoman; John Bensling, son-in-law; Rob. Greene, Wm. Gymmyngham, and me John Hewke, witnesses, Dated 28th May, 1609. Proved 26th July, 1609, by executrix.— Norwich Archd., 1609, fo. 179.

PHILIP TAYLOR of Upton, blacksmith. To be buried in churchyard there; to poor of Upton, 5s.; James, eldest son, lands late uncle Richd. Taylor gave me in Upton,

Fishley, and S. Walsham; Gabriel, youngest son, £40;
Alice, wife (sole executrix), lands bought of Richd. Taylor
my brother, for her life, and then to Christopher, second
son; Elizabeth Taylor, dau., £10; Adam, son, tenement in
Piggings' Gap in Upton, late bought of Edmund Taylor,
my brother. Christr. Athow, Jno. Bullock, yeoman, Jas.
Goat, Mr. Tho. Dyerton, clerk, witnesses. Dated 15th Feb.
8th of James. Proved 18th Feb. 1610, by executrix.—
Norwich Archdy., 1610, fo. 22.

EDMUND TAYLOR of Upton, boteman. To be buried in
churchyard of Upton; Katherine, wife, "she is grievously
and very sore infected," to be set, put, and kept where the
townsmen and minister of Upton wish; John, youngest
son, £15; Luce Taylor, youngest dau., £10; my other
four children, viz., Roger, eldest son; Mary, wife of Tho.
Glozer, my eldest dau.; and Joan Taylor, dau.; and the
other Mary Taylor, my youngest daughter. Henry Daynes,
friend, of Fishley, executor. John Bullock, *the middlemost*,
John Barker, Rob. Gemyngham, jun., and me, Tho. Dyerton,
clerk, witnesses. Dated 13th Feb. 1611. Proved 17th Feb.
1611, by executor. [Note by T. R. T.: he had two daughters
named Mary.]—Norwich Archd., 1611, fo. 339.

31st Aug. 1611. ROBERT TAYLOR, deceased. Admon.
granted to Anne Taylor, the relict.—*Ibid.*

WILLIAM PYNN, the elder, of Upton. Gave to Robert
his son, 21s., and Cassias his daughter, 20s. and a bedstead,
when of age, to be paid by Elizabeth Pynn his daughter,
whom he makes executrix. In presence of Tho. Salter,
Ellen Wythey, wid. Dated 16th Jan. 1612. Proved 17th
Feb. 1612, by executrix at Acle, before Jno. Holt, S.T.B.,
surrogate.—Norwich Archdy., 1612, fo. 240.

WILLIAM TAYLOR, JUN., of Upton, tailor. To be buried
in churchyard of Upton; Henry Daynes of Fishley, my

houses, &c., in Upton; Margaret, wife, £13, and to be sole executrix; James Golt and Robert Grene of Upton to invest £15 for the benefit of Edmond, Anne, and William, "my little children," till the youngest is ten years of age. He bequeaths certain boards of deal, elm, &c., to Henry Daynes. Willm. Taylor, son and heir of Robt. Taylor, Ambrose Clarke, and me Tho. Beston, clk., and others, witnesses. Dated 3rd Feb. 1612. Proved 17th Feb. 1612, at Upton, before Tho. Dyerton, clk., surrogate for Norw. Archdy., by the executrix.—Norwich Archdy., 1612, fo. 226.

REUBEN WYNNE of Upton, labourer. Gave Amy Wynne his daughter certain articles of household, and residue to Agnes his wife. Wm. Goate, John Bullock of Upton, witnesses. Dated month of May, 1612. Proved 19th Oct. 1612, by widow.—Norwich Archdy., 1612, fo. 18.

CHRISTOPHER ATHOWE of Upton, husbandman. To be buried in the church there; to repair of church, 2s. 6d.; to poor, 6s. 8d.; John, son, executor; and Mary, wife of said John; Robert Athowe, grandson; Alice Taylor, widow, daughter. John Baker, John Bullock, James Goate, Thomas Deyrton, clerk, witnesses. Dated 21st Nov. 1614. Proved 20th Nov. 1615.—Norwich Archdeaconry, fo. 580. [No other Upton wills in 1614-5 book.]

EDMUND WETHIE of Upton, yeoman. To be buried in churchyard of Upton. Elizabeth, wife, to be executrix, and to have his houses, &c., till Robert the son is of age, also his tenement called Estons, where Roger Goat now dwells, near Robert Gimingham's; Katherine, daughter, £40, acre at Sweetswonge near John Bullock and Gregory Goate; Margaret Browne, sister, 10s.; Elizabeth, "my sister." Rob. Gymingham, Jno. Houldyn, Ric. Benslinge, John Athow, Christr. Benslinge, Wm. Goate, witnesses. Dated 27th Feb. 1617. Proved 3rd April, 1618, by relict.—Consistory, 1618, fo. 84.

K 2

Upton, 1618, 16th Oct. JOHN TAYLOR, deceased. Admon.
to William Taylor, nephew.—Consistory, Admon., 1605-25.

ANN CHURCH of Upton, singlewoman. Robert Gyming-
ham the elder, of Upton, my brother-in-law, executor.
Andrew Church, brother; Robert Church, bróther; to poor
of Upton, 30*s*.; of Acle, 10*s*.; Blofield, 20*s*. ; and South
Walsham, 10*s*. Property at Hemlington and Blofield. Robt.
Grose, Robert Gymingham, and Edwd. Bond, witnesses.
Dated 15th Nov. 1618. Proved 7th Sept. 1619.—Norwich
Archdeaconry.

RICHARD BENSLYN of Upton. To be buried in churchyard there; to church, 2*s*. 6*d*.; John, son, Horsey property;
Richard, son of said son John. Christopher, son, executor.
Granddaughter, Mary Wethie (daughter of Edmund Wethie,
late of Upton, deceased), aged one year and a half; daughter
Elizabeth Solomon, mother of said Mary Wethie; James
Solomon of Upton, son-in-law, and *father-in-law* (? step-
father) of Mary Wethie ; Katherine Wethie, granddaughter ; Marie Wethie, granddaughter ; Robert Wethie,
grandson ; property at Potter Heigham named. Dated 23rd
March, 1619. Proved 25th April, 1620.—Norwich Archdeaconry.

JAMES GOAT of Upton, yeoman. To be buried in churchyard there; to repair of church, 10*s*.; Mary Goat ; Margaret
Goat ; Hester Goat, eldest daughter ; my daughters to have
use of little house called " The Shop"; John, eldest son;
John Baker, grandson. Mary, my daughter, sole executrix.
Richard Howlett, John Bullock, and John Greenwoode,
witnesses. Dated 16th April, 1625. Proved 18th Oct.
1625.—Norwich Consistory Court, fo. 212.

THOMAS MOWER of Upton, yeoman. To be buried in
churchyard there; Christian, wife, to have his land which
he bought of John Cubitt of Walsham, for her life, and

then to Edmund Mower, son ; Judith, dau., £20. Tho.
More, clerk, Robert Fenn of S. Walsham, executors.
Thomas Mower, John More, and others, witnesses. Dated
18th April, 1630. Proved 3rd May, 1630. More renounced,
admon. issued to the relict.—Norwich Archdy., 1630, fo. 19.

JOHN GREENWOOD of Upton, yeoman. To be buried in
churchyard of Upton ; Mary, wife (sole executrix), lands in
Upton and in Horsey, for life, and to bring up the children ;
then to John, son ; Elizabeth Greenwood, dau., £10 ; Mary
Greenwood, dau., £10. John Bullock, John Creake, and
me Christr. Benslin, witnesses. Dated 15th June, 1630.
Proved 10th July, 1630, by relict.—Norwich Archdy., 1630,
fo. 35.

THOS. CREAKE of Upton, yeoman. Poor of Upton, 20s.;
John, son, copyhold in Upton, Fishley, and S. Walsham,
which he had in reversion and would come to him on death
of Lucie Creake his mother, he to pay Edward, son, £120 ;
Edward, son, land bought of Joan Stones, widow; Amy,
wife ; Ann Benslyn, my wife's dau., a heifer; Judith
Benslyn, sister to said Ann, a heifer. John, son, executor.
Jno. Creake, Vincent Bullock, Rob. Wethie, and me Edw.
Hilton, witnesses. Dated 27th Aug. 1630. Proved 23rd
Sept. 1630, by executor. On 27th Aug. 1630, he sur-
rendered his lands to use of his will, by hands of Vincent
Bullock, copyholder of same manor.—Norwich Archdy.,
1630, fo. 71.

JOHN WYNN, the elder, of Upton, husbandman. To be
buried in parish church of Upton. Son William, sole
executor. Son Christopher. Wm. Gimingham, Christopher
Benslyn, witnesses. Dated 10th Dec. 1630. Proved 20th
July, 1635.—Norwich Archdeaconry, fo. 45.

LUCY CREAKE of Upton, widow. To be buried in parish
churchyard; Edward Creake of Upton, grandson. John

Creake of Upton, grandson, executor. Legacies of household effects. Judith Mower, Christr. Bensling, witnesses. Dated 15th July, 1631. Proved 17th April, 1632, by executor.—Norwich Archdy., 1632, fo. 426.

WILLIAM GOATE of Upton, yeoman. Poor of Upton, 3*s.* 4*d.*; Thomasine, wife (executrix), all his lands, &c., for her life, and then to go to Edward, son, who is to pay each of his brothers and sisters £20. Vincent Bullock, Richd. Lawes, Edwd. Miller, Gregory Goate, witnesses. Dated 1st March, 1636. Proved 27th March, 1637, by widow.—Norwich Archdy., 1637, fo. 169.

THOMAS LINKON, the elder, of Upton. Elizabeth Linkon, granddau., £4 when twenty-one, residue to Andrew, son, who is to be executor. Andrew Church, Tho. Irons, James Norton, witnesses. Dated 3rd Sept. 1639. Proved 18th May, 1640.—Norwich Archdy., 1640, fo. 33.

DANIELL SHANKE of Upton, gent. To poor of Upton, 20*s.*; Elizabeth, wife, lands in Bradwell, Borough Castle, Belton, and Gorleston, she to bring up the children and to pay the legacies of Daniel Shanke, my father; Daniel, eldest son. Wife to be sole executrix. Tho. More, cler., Margt. Wilkins, witnesses. Dated 16th Jan. 1640. Proved 29th Jan. 1640, by widow.—Norwich Archdy., 1640, fo. 138.

JOHN BULLOCK of Upton. Elizth., wife, lands in Upton and Acle for her life, and then to John, son; Katherine, daughter. William, son, executor. Judith Rough, widow, sister, 10*s.* a year for four years; poor of Upton, 5*s.* Danl. Shanke, John Goate, witnesses. Dated 4th April, 1640. Proved 20th April, 1640.—Norwich Archdy., 1640, fo. 14.

JOHN BARKER of Upton, husbandman. Katherine Barker, dau., house where I dwell, and to be sole executrix; Robert, son, lands in Upton; Thomas, son, £5. Daniel Shanke, Richd. Alexander, Charles Greene, Rob. Gimingham, witnesses. Dated 28th May, 1640. Proved 27th July, 1640, by executrix.—Norwich Archdy., 1640, fo. 62.

LUCIE CHURCH, widow, of Upton. Dau., Lucy Church, £8, and to be sole executrix; son-in-law Edmond Bishopp; says she has debts due to her from Robt. Goate of Upton, Gregory Goate of Upton, Andrew Lencon of Upton, and Wm. Goodens, jun., of Burlingham St. Andrew. Andrew Lencon, Jas. Norton, witnesses. Dated 29th Jan., 1640. Proved 5th April, 1641, by executrix.—Norwich Archdy., 1641, fo. 190.

MARGARET WYLKES of Upton, widow. "Whereas my father, Thomas Arnold of Blofield, gave me £35· out of the house where he dwells to be divided after the death of him and his wife between my five daughters and youngest son," leaves them bequests; dau. Mary, dau. Sarah, and two youngest daughters; son John, 40s.; speaks of her six children; John Reve of S. Walsham is indebted to her in sums of money. Christr. Jay of S. Birlingham, Tho. Cory of N. Birlingham, executors. Tho. More, Ric. Alexander, witnesses. Dated 4th June, 1641. Proved 3rd July, 1641, by executors.—Norwich Archdy., 1641, fo. 228.

JOHN HOULDEN of Upton, husbandman. To be buried in churchyard of Upton; Bridget Houlden, dau., a cow; the said cow to be wintered by Christr., son; geese, ducks, and hens to be divided equally between said son and dau. Son, sole executor. Ann Churchman, Christr. Bensling, witnesses. Dated 9th Aug. 1641. Proved 27th Sept. 1641, by executor.—Norwich Archdy., 1641, fo. 289.

ELIZABETH SHANKE of Upton, widow of Daniel Shanke, gent. All his property to be sold and divided between his four daughters; after paying for son Daniel to be bound apprentice, dau. Martha Shanke, £50; three youngest daus., £40 each; two youngest sons, £50 each; son Thomas, son

John, to go to school and then be apprenticed. Brother
Wm. Hickling of Mattishall, John Jesupp of Crostwick near
Norwich, John Goate of Upton, executors. Friend Roger
Reynalls of Lingwood, gent., supervisor. Robt. Gymingham,
Willm. Bullock, witnesses. Dated 18th April, 1642. Proved
23rd April, 1642, by Hickling and Jessopp, power reserved
to Goate.—Norwich Archdy., 1642, fo. 319.

JOHN CREAKE, SEN., of Upton, yeoman. Bartholomew
Creake, son, his houses, &c.; Robert Creake, son, 20s.;
Mary Creake, dau., 10s.; Ann Creake, dau., 10s. Joane,
wife, sole executrix. Edwd. Packe, Walter Peeke, Wm.
Bullock, Christr. Bensling, witnesses. Dated 14th July, 1642.
Proved 17th Sept. 1642, by widow.—Norwich Archdy., 1642,
fo. 354.

JAMES BENSLYNG of Upton, yeoman. To be buried in
Upton; poor there, 6s.; poor of Acle, 10s.; Robert, son,
messuage in Upton I bought of Wm. Gait and Judith his
wife, late Adam Taylor's; lands at Turfenn in Upton, Normarsh in Upton, White Carr in Upton, Great Fen in
Upton, Hansell Grene in Upton; Robt. and John Bensling,
grandchildren; Margaret Bensling, dau.-in-law; William,
son; James Bensling, grandson; Ann Bensling, granddau.;
Robert Bensling, grandson; Jno. Bensling, grandson; Eliz.
Bensling, granddau.; Margaret, wife. Sons Robt. and Willm.
to be executors. Rob. Greene, Jno. Creake, Jas. Taylor, Jno.
Goate, Christr. Bensling, Vincent Bullock, witnesses. Dated
12th April, 1643. Proved 21st June, 1643, by sons.—Norwich
Archdy., 1643, fo. 434.

THOMAS MORE of Upton, clarke. Ann, wife, house where
I dwell and all other property; to pay his four children,
John, Thomas, Phylemon, and Abra, £10 each, and give
his daughters, Ann Holden and Elizabeth Golt, each a silver
spoon, and to be sole executrix. Christr. Bensling, Richd.

Goate, witnesses. Dated 29th Oct. 1646. Proved 17th July, 1647, by executrix.—Consistory, 1647, fo. 59.

EDMUND FISHER of Upton, carpenter. To be buried in churchyard there; Lydia, wife, houses and marshes, and to be sole executrix; John, son; Robert, son of Richard Fisher, to have legacy after his mother's decease; Robert Fisher, grandson; Robert, son. Robert Goat, John Goat, John Bullock, witnesses, Dated 1st May, 1646. Proved 14th Sept. 1650.—Fo. 333.

EDMUND FISHER of Upton, carpenter. To be buried in churchyard there; Lidia, wife, house where I dwell, and to be executrix; John, son; Robert, son of Richard Fisher, 20s.; mentions Puttock dole, Rush dole called Southhold, on way from Upton to Normarsh; Rob. Goate, John Goate, John Bullock, and others, witnesses. Dated 5th May, 1646. Proved 14th Sept., 1650, and admon. granted to John the son, the executrix having died before testator.—Norwich Archd., 1630, fo. 333.

WILLIAM BULLOCK of Upton, yeoman. Eldest son William to have house where he dwelt; second son John, £40; youngest son Robert, £40. Susan, wife, sole executrix. Rob. Gymingham, Ann Bensling, witnesses. Dated 5th May, 1647. Proved 30th Oct. 1647, by executrix—Norwich Archdy., 1647, fo. 350.

CHRISTOPHER HOLDEN of Upton, Norfolk. Legacies to Abery Houlden, my eldest child; Mary Houlden, second dau.; Ann Houlden, third dau.; John Willeses two children, Mary Wills and Margaret Wills, 20s. each. Andrew Manthorp, Thomas Last, executors. Hercules Gout, supervisor. Aide Eadge, Robt. Goate, witnesses. Dated 6th Oct. 1647. Proved 30th Oct. 1647, by executors.—Norwich Archdy., 1647, fo. 299.

VINCENT BULLOCK of Upton, yeoman. To be buried in

churchyard of Upton; to poor of Upton, 20s.; Robert Feen, grandson; Margaret and Sampson Feen, grandchildren; Christopher Bullock, youngest son, tenement in Upton; Margaret Creake, widow, cousin, 40s.; two sons, John and Christopher, to divide his moveables equally, and to be executors. John Goat, Robt. Goat, Rob. Gymyngham, and others, witnesses. Dated 12th Dec. 1647. Proved 29th Jan. 1647, by sons. Many lands and abbuttals given.—Norwich Archdy., 1647, fo. 350.

JUDITH GOAT of Upton, widow. Mathew (*sic*) Goat, Philip (*sic*) Goat, Judith Goat, daughters, to have her tenements in Upton, and be executrices; Thomas Blacke, £4 when 21; Nics., £4; Mary, £4; Willm., £4; John, £4; (no relationship given of these Blackes); Ann Ducker, Eliz. Ducker, Frans. Ducker, Wm. Ducker, grandchildren, £10 each when 21; William Ducker, father of the above. This will was put in writing by Christr. Bensling, and read to testatrix in presence of Edmond Taylor, 18th Aug. 1650. Proved 24th Aug. 1650, by the three daughters.—Norwich Archd., 1650, fo. 328.

EDWARD CREAKE of Upton, Norfolk. Helen, daughter, property in Fishley, abutting on Tho. Green's land; Mary Creake, dau., property having Walter Peeke on S., Rob. Gymyngham on E., Edw. Mileham, gent., on E., late John Hill's; Lucy Creake, dau., property having Saml. Hincks, clerk, on E., way leading to the windmill on E.; John, son, property having Anthony Wynn, N. and S., way from Upton to N. Burlingham, W.; child wife is with, provided for. Loving brother John Creake, executor; Thomas, son; Helen, wife, executrix. Sampson Fenn, John Bullocke, John More, witnesses. Dated 15th March, 1651. Proved 22nd Sept. 1652.—Norwich Archdy., 1652, fo. 515.

EDWARD CREAKE of Upton. Helen, dau., lands in

Fishley; Mary Creake, dau.; Lucy Creake, dau.; John, son; child my wife is withal, £20; Helen, wife, and brother John Creake, certain lands, &c., to bring up the children till son Thomas is 21. Said Helen and John to be executors. Sampson Fenn, Jno. Bullocke, Jno. Moore, witnesses. Dated 15th March, 1651. Proved 23rd Sept. 1652, by both exors.—Norwich Archd., 1652, fo. 515.

CHARLES GREEN of Upton, husbandman. Charles, second son, tenement adjoining Lincoln's yard, where I dwell; John, eldest son, 5s.; Joan, wife, executrix; two youngest daughters, Susan Green and Ellen Green; Willm., son of Willm. Bullock, deceased; says he has £25 in the hands of John Goat, sen., of Upton, yeoman, due after decease of Ann Goat, wife of Edmond Goat of Limpenhoe. John Goate, Henry Harplie, Walter Peeke, Robert Goate, senr., witnesses. Dated 8th Nov. 1651. Proved 6th Dec. 1651, by the relict.—Norwich Archd., 1651, fo. 335.

SUSAN, wife of WALTER PEEKE of Upton. Divided her household goods amongst the three sons which she had by her first husband, Wm. Bullock, viz., William, John, and Robert Bullock; and Margaret, Ann, Susan, and Sarah, daughters of Walter Peeke aforesaid. Ann Nunne, Cattaring Barber, witnesses. Dated 9th May, 1652. Proved 14th May, 1652. And admon. granted to said Walter Peeke the husband, during the minority of the said three sons.— Consistory, 1652, fo. 115.

JOHN CREAKE of Upton, yeoman. Robert, eldest son; Edward, son; John, son; Christopher, son; Susan Creake, daughter; Mary Creake, daughter; Rachel, wife. James, second son, sole executor. Poor of Upton, 20s. Dated 6th Feb. 1655. Proved 27th Feb. 1655.—Norwich Archdeaconry.

JOHN BAKER of Upton, Norf., yeoman. Sister Strangellman,

£30; Francis Baker, £10; Jesper Danford, £10; Susan Danford, my sister's dau., £10; directs his legacies to be paid in church porch of Framlingham Castle, Suffolk. Rob. Danford, Richard Smith, junr., Framlingham, exors. Daniel Rayner, Susan Smyth, Tho. Irons, witnesses. Dated 18th Feb. 1656. Proved 17th April, 1661.—Consistory, Regr. for 1661, fo. 567.

The nuncupative will of BARNEY SHEPHEARD of Upton, in the county of Norff., clerke—I bequeath my soule into the hands of Allmighty God, hoping, by and through the meritts of my blessed Saviour, of a joyfull resurrection at the last day, and my body to the ground, from whence it came, desiring to have Christian buriall; also I give unto Elizabeth Shepheard, my daughter, all my reall and personall estate wheresoever for ever. And I earnestly desire that her grandmother, my mother-in-law, Abra Moundford, would take care in the bringing up and educatinge this my poore daughter with the profitts & revenews of the said estate, which she hath faithfully promised to doe this twentieth day of February, 1657.

This declaracõn or will was made and declared by the said Mr. Barney Shepheard, the twentieth day of February, 1657, being in his perfect minde and memory, in the presence and hearing of us whose names are here under written—

The mark of James Norton,
The mark of Lucy Byrde.

11th March, 1657 (English style), administration of all and singular the goods and chattels of BARNEY SHEPHEARD, clerke, late deceased, with his nuncupative will annexed, was, by the Judges at London, granted to Abra Moundford, grandmother by the mother's side, of Elizabeth Shepheard, the only daughter of the said deceased, and universal

legatee in the said will: she, the said Abra Moundford,
being testamentary guardian of the said Elizabeth during
her minority : she, the said Abra Moundford, being in due
forme of law sworn well and truly to administer.—Prerogative
Court of Canterbury. Copy preserved in a book belonging
to Norwich Archdeaconry (1653-60), fo. 405.

ROBERT GREENE, SENIOR, of Upton, yeoman. Poor of
Upton, 10s.; poor of Acle, 10s. ; Robert and John, sons ;
Robert, son of son John ; Mary Greene, dau. of son John ;
Edward, son of Henry Mack ; Nicholas, Eliz., and Martha,
children of Hy. Mack ; Tho. Goate, son of Christr., god-
son. Mary, wife, sole executrix. Dated 16th Dec. 1647.
Proved 15th July, 1657, at London. Copy in Norw. Arch.
fo. 335, 1653-60.

JOHN BULLOCKE of Upton, yeoman. Vincent, son,
tenement purchased of Rob. Wythy, in Upton ; Elizabeth,
dau., land in a furlong called Huntingdon, between the
land of the lord of the manor W., land of Geo. Bird, Esq.,
E., and the manor S. and N. ; Charles, son. Marable,
wife, executrix. Poor of Upton, 20s. Dated 21st Jan.
1658. Proved 9th Mar. 1658, at London. Copy in
Norw. Arch., fo. 584, 1653-60.

HENRY HARPLEY of Upton, yeoman. Thomas, eldest
son, house where I dwell, and one acre of arable land
in Sweetsong, between lands of George Bird, Esq., on
north, of Robert Greene south, and on Geo. Bird east.
Mary, wife, sole executrix. John, youngest son, two and
a half acres of arable land at Sweetsong, between land
of Wm. Cobbe north, Christopher Gymingham south, and
George Bird east ; one acre between Thomas Greene north,
Edward Mileham east, divers men west ; half acre between
Ed. Mileham east and west, and Robert Benslyn south.
Anne Harpley, dau., one acre and a half of arable land,

late purchased of William Allen. Dated 16th Feb. 1662. Proved 23rd May, 1663.—Norw. Arch., fo. 257.

EDWARD GOATE of Upton, yeoman. To the poor of Burlingham St. Edmund, 5*s.*; to the poor of Upton, 21*s.*; James Barne ; Margaret Worledge, sister ; Elizabeth Gillians, daughter of said Margaret; Mary Worledge, ditto; Joan Worledge, ditto; Dorothy Worledge, ditto; Edward Cooke of Upton, son of William; Susan Cooke of Upton, daughter of William ; Edward, son of Robert Goate, brother; Elizabeth, daughter of Robert Goate, brother. Brother Robert, executor. Dated 10th Feb. 1663. Proved 11th Sep. 1665.—Consistory Court, Liber Stockedell, fo. 12.

ROBERT GOATE of Upton, yeoman. Poor of Upton, 20*s.*; poor of Acle, 20*s.*; poor of South Walsham, 20*s.*; sister Margaret Worlidge; Edward, son; late brother Edward ; Elizabeth, daughter; "child my wife is withal." Elizabeth, wife, sole executrix. Thomas Skinner and John Greenewood, supervisors of will. Dated 5th Sept. 1665. Proved 11th Sept. 1665.—Consistory Court, Liber Stockedell, fo. 7.

WILLIAM TOMPSON of Upton, husbandman. To be buried in churchyard there ; Lucy his wife to have all and be sole executrix. Dated 24th May, 1637. Proved 2nd Nov. 1644.—Norw. Archd., fo. 71.

CHRISTOPHER CREIKE of Upton, singleman, being sick, &c. Mary Creike, my sister, all my estate, and executrix. Mr. Matthew Goodwin of Acle, Danl. Creike of Upton, Sarah, wife of Edward Fisher of Upton, carpenter, being witnesses. Dated 26th Jan. 1672. Proved 26th Feb. 1672, by executrix.—Consistory, original will No. 49, 1672, not copied in the register.

JOHN MORE of Upton, being sick, &c. Gave 10*s.* to John, eldest son, and household effects to Robert More his youngest son, whom he made executor. Judith Robinson,

witness. Dated 16th April, 1672. Proved 8th Nov. 1672.
—Consistory, original will No. 41, 1672, not in the
register.

JOHN GREENE of Upton, yeoman. To be buried in the
church of Upton; Sarah, wife, £20, to be paid in Corton
parish church porch, Suffolk; land bought of Edwd. Goate
of Buddedell, and William Bullock of Upton; Mary, dau.,
wife of John Jaye, my house in Leystoft; John, son;
Elizabeth, dau., wife of Joseph Littlewood, £50; Mary
Littlewood, dau. of said Joseph, granddau.; Mary, dau.;
Edward, son, £100. Robert, son, sole executor. Rob.
Greene, Ric. Fiske, Jno. Curtis, witnesses. Dated 7th July,
1672. Proved 9th Sept. 1672, by executor. Codicil dated
15th July, 1672, but no fresh names in it.—Consistory,
original will No. 52 in 1672 bundle, not copied into the
register.

ROBERT GOODWYN of Upton, vicker. Being sick in
body, &c.; to Robert, my son, 10s.; to Bethell, my son, 10s.;
to Walter, my son, half the amount of my stock when
priced ; to John, my son, residuary legatee and sole executor.
Joseph Burre, Ann Pett, Robert Greene, witnesses. Robt.
Goodwyn. Dated 21st Jany. 1678. Proved 1st March,
1678.—Consistory, original will, No. 106 in 1678 parcel.

JOSEPH LITTLEWOOD of Upton, yeoman. Being very
weak, &c., left all to his two daughters, Mary and Elizabeth.
He desired William Cobb of Upton, to be his executor, but
"Mr. Styles, who writt this, was called away," having
omitted to set down Cobb as executor, and before he came
back, testator was senseless. No date, but witnesses, Jno.
Goodwyn, Gabriel Chapman, Martha Pitt, who were
sworn to truth of above, 16th Nov. 1680.—Consistory,
Register 1680, fo. 169.

JOHN EMPEROR of Upton. Mary and Elizabeth his

sisters, to have his property in Yarmouth, Upton, and Ludham. Dated 23rd Nov. 1680. Proved 15th Dec. 1680.—Norw. Archd., fo. 322.

MARIE FISHER of Vpton, widow. William Smith of Onsby to have all she had, and be sole executor. Wm. Cobb, John Goodwyn, Elizth. Davy, witnesses. Dated 19th Jan. 1681. Proved 20th Jan. 1681 (next day). (Marks woman, no signature).—Consistory, original, No. 56 of 1681 parcel.

JOHN READ of Upton. Administration granted 20th Jan. 1685, to Abrye Read, relict; Thomas Harpley of Upton, yeoman; and John Harpley of Upton, singleman; by Consistory Court.

JAMES BENSLYNGE of Upton. Administration, Norwich Archdeaconry, 16th Aug. 1675, to Deborah, relict. Rd. Fiske of Upton, lanius, and Robt. Thompson of Upton, blacksmith, bondsmen.

EDWARD GOATE of Upton, yeoman. Mary, wife, to have his lands in Upton, Acle, Clippesby, Fishley, and S. Walsham, for life, and then to go to Robert, son, who is to pay to his sisters, Elizabeth Goate, dau., and Mary Goate, dau., " my two daughters," £50 each. Tho. Coates of Acle, gent., has a mortgage of testator's. Tho. Coates, Edw. Cooke, Christr. Gimmingham, Tho. Hall, witnesses. Dated 18th July, 1692. Proved 14th Jany., 169⅞.—Consistory, 1692, fo. 135.

SAMUEL JERMY of Upton, Norfolk, yeoman. Mary, eldest daughter of Samuel Jermy of Southwood; Roger Jermy of Surlingham; Hannah, daugh. of Edmund Jermy, my late brother, deceased; Samuel Jermy and Jno. Jermy, sons of Jno. Jermy, my kinsman, late of Reedham, deceased; Ann Yallop, daugh. of brother Roger Jermy, deceased; children of Saml. Jermy of Southwood; Susan, wife (residue), and executrix. Dated 29th April, 1722. Proved 12th May, 1722.—Consistory Court, 1722, fo. 26.

HENRY NELSON of Upton, clerk. Henry, son, £5; Ann, wife, executrix, and to bring up Ann, daughter; Marmaduke Forster, jun., Sarah Cater, witnesses. Dated 29th Oct., 1723. Proved 6th Nov., 1723, by executrix.—Consistory Court, 1723, fo. 205.

ELIZABETH GIMINGHAM of Upton, Norfolk. Grandson Christopher Riches, a rood of land in Upton; four grand-children, Ann Church, Eliz. Riches, John Riches, Christr. Riches; mentions her house on Cartgate Green; Margaret Cater, daughter, 2s. 6d., and if she be left a widow, to have her dwelling in part of my house; Simon Riches, grandson. Simon Riches, son-in-law, executor. Geo. Docking and Edward Tomson, witnesses. Dated 26th Jan,, 1723. Proved 6th June, 1724, by executor.—Consistory Court, 1724, fo. 82.

THOMAS DAY of Upton, cordwainer. Henry Day, his father; John, son of Thomas Day, his father's brother's son. Thomas Day, father's brother's son, executor. Simeon Riches, Susan Bishop, and Martha Parkins, witnesses. Dated 19th April, 1731. Proved 8th Aug., 1731.—Norwich Archdeaconry, No. 127, fo. 289.

WILLIAM ROGERS of Upton, bricklayer. Daughter Elizabeth Rogers; close in Upton, late purchased of Robert Cubitt, and the close late purchased of Wm. Wynn; a pightle called "Jibbs"; land in Upton, near Woollestab, purchased of Tho. Diamond, deceased. Robert Goate of Upton, Gent., supervisor of will. Wife, in lieu of all thirds, &c., as per my bond to James Jay. William Rogers, son, executor. 10s. to parson of Upton, for a funeral sermon. Rebecca Jay, Ann Docking, Jere. Berry, witnesses. Dated 6th Mar., 1731. Proved 11th Mar., 173½.—Norwich Arch-deaconry, fo. 323.

L

HENRY HOBARD of Upton, yeoman. Mary, wife; James
Hobard of Hemblington, brother; Thomas Hobard of
Upton, wheelwright, brother; Mary, wife of Joseph Madley
of Martham, sister; John, son of brother Thomas; John
Hobard's two children; property in Upton and S. Walsham.
Dated 31st Mar., 1740. Proved 24th May, 1740.

JOHN JAY of Upton, yeoman. Anne, wife, executrix.
James, son; Christopher, son. James Skynner, cousin, of
Upton, executor. Dated 11th Feb., 1703. Proved 8th July,
1704.

SUSAN BISHOP of Upton, singlewoman. Left her copyholds to her kinsman, James Hubbert of Thirne, son of
Thomas Hubbert of Upton; Elizabeth Bishop, her brother's
child; Henry Hubbert, brother of said James; Margaret
Hubbert, sister of said James; Susan Hubbert, ditto; Mary
Hubbert, ditto. Dated 2nd Aug., 1762. Proved 17th June,
1766.—Norwich Archdeaconry.

ANNA LITTLEWOOD of Upton, widow. Ann, daughter of
Stephen Child of Wymondham, cordwainer, and Anna, his
wife, my daughter; Enoch Littlewood, son, executor; Amy,
wife of John Mitchells; Margaret, my daughter, wife of
Geo. Docking. Dated 18th Sept., 1762. Proved 22nd Nov.,
1783.—Norwich Archdeaconry.

Marriage licences granted by the Bishop of Norwich.
1565, 20th Sept. Edward Wightman of Burnham Norton
and Elizabeth Ossent, to be married at Upton.

Marriage licence by Bishop of Norwich, 20th May, 1585.
Richard Cammell of Upton, waterman, and Cecily Gould
of same place, spinster. (General licence, no place.)

Marriage licence, 21st Dec., 1585, Bishop of Norwich. Willm. Wynne of Upton, yeoman, and Margaret Browne of same, spinster. (General licence.)

ADDENDA.

The Solemn League and Covenant. The following interesting note occurs in the Consignation Book, 1662, Bishop's Registry, shewing that the Vicar appointed on the Restoration of Charles II. renounced the Solemn League and Covenant.

"Upton. Robt. Goodwin ord. priest by Hy., Bp. of Cicestr., 15 Dec., 1660, inst^d by Edwd, Bp. Nor., at present (presentation) of Matt., Bp. of Ely, 17 Dec., 1661, test sup renūncon solemn fœdus p eune, 22 Aug., 1662."

A Will of 1383. The earliest will of a Vicar, found by Mr. Tallack, is that of John Smalewood de Beketon.

JOHN, perpetual Vicar of the church of Upton. To be buried in the cemetery of Upton; to emendation of the said church, 16s. 8d.; to sustentation of light of B. Mary in said church, 3s. 4d.; to emendation of church of Weybrede, 6s. 8d.; to emendation of church of Beketon,

6s. 8d.; Thomas, my brother, 6s. 8d.; Margaret Bond, 6s. 8d.; Thomas, son of Matilda, my sister, 6s. 8d.; Beatrix, dau. of Thomas, my brother, 6s. 8d.; Felicia, wife of Adam Mey, 2s.; to emendation of church of Fysschelee for soul of Nicholas quondam rector dictæ eccliæ, 6s. 8d.; to John Sepater, rector of said church, 2s.; Thomas Person, four bushels of barley; William Smyth of Upton, four bushels of barley; John Carter, four bush. barley; Henry Smyth, four bush. barley; Julian Godknape, 6s. 8d.; John de Dylham, 6s. 8d.; to William Ker, unum portiforium cum magna vestura; to Dominus Willm de Beketon, unum portiforium cum serico co-opertum; Alice Warner, 6s. 8d.; residue to disposal of executors whom he appoints; William, Vicar of Weybrede; Willm, Vicar of church of Wodebastwyk; and John Fuller, of Upton. Dated die dom^{ca} in festo Sci Francisci, 1383. Proved 9th Oct., 1383—Consistory, Reg. Harsyk, fol. 6.

Sixpence a day. A lease of the Rectory of Upton (in the possession of Mr. Rye) was made July 11th, 1664, between Matthew, Bishop of Ely, and Edmund Witherly, of Norwich, gentleman, and Philip Jenkenson, of St. Andrew's, Holborn, gentleman. The previous lessee was William Hewen, Doctor of Laws. The rent fixed in the lease was £12 per annum. The advowson of the Vicarage was excepted and reserved to the Bp. of Ely; "also an allowance of sixpence p^r diem intended to be made to the Vicar of Upton."

The lessees further covenant every quarter-day to "pay and satisfy, or cause to be paid and satisfied, unto the Vicar of the parish church of Upton aforesaid (who shall be thereunto lawfully instituted by the Bishop of Norwich for the time being) sixpence p^r diem for every day in the preceding quarter if ye same shall be lawfully demanded." In the event of a Vicar not being lawfully appointed, or the Vicarage being void, "the allowance of sixpence p^r diem" to be paid to the Bishop of Ely.

The Perk Light.

To the list of Ancient Lights kept burning in Upton Church in pre-Reformation times, given at p. 54, should be added the Perk Light, which was the Roodscreen Light.

Elizabethan Cups.

After the restoration of the Cup to the laity in the Holy Communion, the small but exquisite chalices left in the Parish Churches by Edward VI.'s Commissioners were superseded in Queen Elizabeth's reign by large Cups; of which that described at p. 60 is an example. The following extract from the Archdeacon's Register throws some light upon the excessive quantity of wine provided for one Celebration of the Holy Communion, and suggests a reason for the capacity of these Elizabethan Cups.

"Upton. Jo. Bullock et Robert Greene no^r, for

that they did not p̄vide sufficient bread for Cōnon, so that xij or xiiij went away without breade, xiiij daie March, 1606."

In replying to this charge, the Churchwardens appear to have ordered bread, "and vij pynts of wyne for the sayd commuñ, and there were but xlvij cōmcants, and they suppose there was no want of bread for the comⁿ, howsoeuer the same was ordered and there."

The Census. The Census of 1891 shews a slight increase in the population of Upton. Inhabited houses, 111 ; uninhabited houses, 11 ; males, 251 ; females, 261 ; total, 512. This does not include Fishley.—See p. 100.

Corrections. On page 50, for "*British Archæological Journal for 1890*," read "*Archæological Journal*, vol. xlvi., 1889."

On page 71, for "*vide* his will, page '121," read "page 141."

INDEX OF PERSONS.

INDEX OF PLACES.

FIELD AND OTHER LOCAL NAMES
IN WILLS.

SURNAMES IN MONUMENTAL
INSCRIPTIONS AND WILLS.

AGAS GOOSE, PRINTER, RAMPANT HORSE STREET, NORWICH.

LaVergne, TN USA
01 September 2009

156661LV00003B/95/A